# FLIP YOUR FOCUS

IGNITING PEOPLE, PROFITS AND
PERFORMANCE THROUGH
UPSIDE-DOWN LEADERSHIP

Bob Spiel

Copyright © 2017 by Bob Spiel.

All rights reserved. No part of this publication may be reproduced, distributed or transmitted in any form or by any means, including photocopying, recording, or other electronic or mechanical methods, without the prior written permission of the publisher, except in the case of brief quotations embodied in critical reviews and certain other noncommercial uses permitted by copyright law. For permission requests, write to the publisher, addressed "Attention: Permissions Coordinator," at the address below.

Bob Spiel
68 N 800 E
Lindon, UT 84042
www.flipyourfocusbook.com

Editor's note: In some cases, names and identifying details have been changed to protect the privacy of those involved.

Ordering Information:
Quantity sales. Special discounts are available on quantity purchases by corporations, associations, and others. For details, contact the "Special Sales Department" at the address above.

Flip Your Focus
Igniting People, Profits and Performance through Upside-Down Leadership/ Bob Spiel. —1st ed.
ISBN-13: 978-1544765419

# Contents

The Silent Cry for Help ................................................................. 1

Tackle Demands and Tame the Chaos by Becoming an Upside-Down Leader ................................................................................ 11

Flipping Your Focus—Thinking Like an Upside-Down Leader ......... 25

Upside-Down Leaders Cast Aside Blame and Take Personal Responsibility .... 41

Let Go of the Past and Challenge Your Limiting Beliefs ...................... 49

Delegate (Almost) Everything — But Vision, Direction, and Pace .......... 63

A Total Commitment to Your Team's Success ..................................... 75

The Power of Clear Expectations, Coupled with Accountability ............ 85

Creating a Culture of Participation and Ownership ............................ 99

What Keeps the Magic Going—Appreciation and Recognition .............. 109

Culture by Design: Building Something That Is Truly Sustainable ......... 117

The Unselfish Organization: What Does Ultimate Success Look Like? ..... 127

Epilogue: The Case for Leadership ..................................................... 137

## TESTIMONIALS ABOUT THE POWER OF FLIP YOUR FOCUS:

"Flip your focus not only includes what a truly great leader provides- setting the course, shaping direction, creating a compelling vision, and setting the pace - but also what they need to be, which is one who CARES! It's not only what a leader does, but how they do it. Bob has taught us this in a wonderfully easy to read, and even easier to apply, format. I recommend it to all who want to truly lead their organization!"

**Lewis L. (Lee) Bird**

CEO of At Home Group Inc.

"Bob Spiel's unique leadership method is revolutionary. His depth and wisdom is both evident and inspiring. Instantly, dramatically improve your life by changing your perspective through diving into his book."

**Grace Rizza**

Founder & CEO Identity Dental Marketing

"Leadership makes the difference between a mediocre company and a great company. It is the bottom line to success. Bob Spiel's personal approach to leadership combines the truths of both research and practicality into usable lessons to organize chaos, improve productivity, and reduce stress. Bob provides practical coaching recommendations that translate leadership principles into action steps for you and your organization."

**Cathy Jameson, PhD**

Founder and CEO Jameson Management
Author, Creating a Healthy Work Environment

"Bob Spiel is a true professional. I've had the pleasure of working alongside him, and he is without a doubt an exemplary leader. He has real experience working with owners and teams at the highest level, and knows how to get results. The principles in this book are sound and founded on experience from the trenches. Bob has

a passion for this work and it shows in this offering. Upside down leadership IS the way to greater results both in and out of every organization."
**Art McCracken**

Chief Performance Officer
LuLaRoe


"Real leaders are rare indeed. In your hands, you hold a blueprint for leading your people in times of challenge and change. Keep this book within arms' reach and refer to it often. It will change the way you think, act and make decisions. Count me a fan!"
**Mark LeBlanc, CSP**

President and CEO, LeBlanc Inc.
Author of Never Be The Same and Growing Your Business!


"Bob Spiel gets it! 'Flip your Focus' has an actionable model that you can apply right now on your journey to becoming a better leader that delivers better results by empowering better relationships."
**Cory Bouck**, Asia-Pacific Business Director, Johnsonville Sausage

Author of The Lens of Leadership: Being the Leader Others WANT to Follow


"If you want a more successful business and a more rewarding work/life balance, this is a must read. Upside-Down leadership is the remedy to so many business and quality of life ills; not just because Bob Spiel says so but, rather, as a result of my own implementation of the principles he so compellingly describes. Thank you, Bob, for sharing something I can actually utilize as the leader of a large and complex organization."
**Sean D. Reyes**

Utah Attorney General


"Clarity and inspiration are the cornerstones of great communication and power-ful leadership. Bob Spiel's new book provides both in spades. He's outlined clear and practical steps and provided massive inspiration to take them. A must read for any leader looking to empower people, strengthen organizations, and leave a legacy of success. Upside Leadership is required reading for my clients and my own leader- ship bible for growing my company and my people from the bottom up!" **Katherine Eitel Belt**

President LionSpeak, Inc.

"After reading Bob Spiel's book, I now understand, in print, what I had always witnessed him doing in practice; Bob could bring opposing board members to a decision, calm the chaos at a company and tame the inner demons of any entrepreneur. Bob is a start to finish, top shelf business adviser with the experience and intellectual basis to craft strategic planning and in-depth performance processes. Class acts that produce results on his level are rare."
**Isaac Jacobsen**

CEO and Founder Accelerate Ventures

"Leadership is about creating an environment where others can learn, perform, and achieve desired results. Bob Spiel shares his experience and his insights in a manner that enables you to move from "knowing" to "doing" as a "flipped" business leader. Using his practical ideas, useful examples, and responding in writing to the Coach's Challenge questions will enable you to understand how you show up as a leader. From this enlightened perspective, you can make magic happen in your own context."
**MJ Hall, MBA, PhD**

Executive, American Society for Training and Development
Author of Designing WorkLearn Networks: Making Magic Happen with Your Profession

"I love the topic of **LEADERSHIP!** Over my career I have read or listened to hundreds of books, articles and speeches on the topic of leadership. Never however, have I heard this topic dissected and laid out in such an easy fashion that **ANY BUSINESS OWNER,** after reading Bob's book, can reach their ultimate level of success.

*Bob's book is not a read and give away book or read and add to the bookshelf book...It is a **TOTAL GUIDE** with each chapter ending with the "**Coaches Challenge**". If you are tired of feeling defeated as a leader and you are tired of hearing your colleagues complain about this very issue of getting those on their team ignited to be the BEST, order your own book and one for your ten best friends! Your life and theirs will change for the better by about 1000%."*
**Linda Miles**, Founder Linda Miles & Associates

Founder, Speaking Consulting Network
Co Founder, Oral Cancer Cause.org
Co Founder, Ultimate Team Mastery

*"Centuries ago, Lao Tzu said, "Of a great leader it is said by his people, 'we did it ourselves.'" In his book, Bob provides some powerful insights and useful tools for releasing the potential of individuals and teams, by "flipping" the role of the leader. You will enjoy both his ideas and his practical coaching methods."*
**Kevin R. Miller**

President, VisionBound International

*"In a must read for the aspiring leader Bob Spiel articulates and illustrates a core truth: great leaders don't build businesses; they build great people. Great leaders don't rule from commanding heights, but by capturing hearts and minds through vision, unity and mentorship of individuals and teams."*
**Matt Sanders**

Vice President
TSC EcoSolutions

*To Judene, for her absolute love and support.*

*To Jim, who believed, and gave more than ever deserved.*

*And, to emerging leaders everywhere.*

INTRODUCTION

Like many entering business today, my early approach to leadership was what had been modeled around me: the top down, control model. With a dad who was retired Navy, it wasn't hard to see this model at work. It seemed to create short term compliance – but under the surface, resentment built and results faltered over time. As a youth, I often wondered if there was another way; a way to enlist the talents of those around you to create something bigger than could ever be dreamed of. This book attempts to capture that journey of finding "another way" – a "flipped" way that creates remarkable success for you, because the team around you is succeeding as well.

This journey would not have been possible without a host of incredible mentors along the way. These were genuine leaders who knew their job was bigger than the bottom line. They were driven to teach, coach, create other leaders and let them run with their roles and responsibilities. They also frequently pointed to mentors in their lives who had lit a fire in their soul – and then commissioned them to light this same fire in others.

Leadership is the greatest force in the world. Whenever history shows a tectonic shift, there has always been leadership at work. It will always be this way as well. As people, we respond to genuine leadership because of our intrinsic desire to be a part of something bigger than ourselves, and our willingness to follow another because of how it makes us feel about ourselves. Given this, there has never been a more important time for a generation of genuine "Upside-down Leaders" to be learn the art of human engagement. There is chaos all around us in business, in our homes, and political institutions; and this dynamic seems to be growing. Yet, the fundamentals have not changed. Vision, clarity, focus, service, ownership, personal responsibility, and unselfishness, are timeless principles that create dramatic human momentum – and life changing result in business and personally.

What this book lacks in empirical evidence, it makes up for in the laboratory of the lives and leaders presented. It is not meant to be a thesis or a research study on the topic. There are entire libraries that can fulfill that desire. Rather, it is written to present radically simple ideas in a simply radical way – to create within leaders everywhere a new vision for what their role truly is.

My eternal thanks go to these wonderful mentors who took the time to teach. They changed everything. I now hope this book will light in others what they lit in me – and that the counsel they gave will be as game changing to the readers today as it was when they first shared their hearts with me.

Bob Spiel
Idaho Falls, ID
March 2017
Flipyourfocusbook.com

CHAPTER ONE

# The Silent Cry for Help

Nothing in life brings us more face-to-face with ourselves than owning a business. Not even sports, schooling, marriage, or raising children cause us to confront who we are; the strengths and weaknesses we possess and what drives us quite like business ownership. It acts as the perfect amplifier of our skills, motivations, self-awareness, thirst for knowledge, ability to communicate, tenacity, planning, leadership, and team-building abilities *because there is no such thing as a no-fault business.*

Consequently, the demands placed on business owners are huge. And this is never more true than in growing a small business where the title of CEO can soon mean "chief everything officer." As customers are gained and employees are hired, an owner's plate becomes increasingly full and is at risk of overflowing. Indeed, with so much pressure and time constraints, all too often important aspects of running a business are neglected: expectations are unclear, accountability is weak, feedback and appreciation are lacking, systems are created by default, what was once simple becomes more and more complex—and it appears the only way to confront these dynamics is to tighten the grip even more. Employees then fall into two camps: over-performers who are burnt out and unhappy, and underperformers who are entitled and unhappy. Along with the ever-constant cash flow worries, there is the fear of failure and—paradoxically—the fear of success. The mounting stress cannot even be escaped at home, but is only momentarily numbed through mindlessly surfing the web or watching a sitcom late in the evening. It seems there is never enough time or energy to get everything done. The hope that launched the business seems to fade into the background as the personal and organizational stressors grow. In the pain of survival comes a cry from within: "I want my life back!"

**Who Is This For?**

This book is written primarily for successful small business owners with growing teams and growing demands who, in very painful moments, have found themselves crying out in the deep recesses of their hearts, "Help! I'm stuck and I don't know how to get unstuck. I can't go back, but I can't go forward the way things are now." This is a critical point and one that I have discovered allows us to become teachable and reachable. When the pain of remaining on the path we are on seems greater than the pain of changing directions, that is a very sacred moment in life and a true tipping point. Here genuine growth can take place as we exercise the human capacity to master new ways of thinking, choose our future, and not be held hostage by the past. There is a Chinese proverb that says, "When the student is ready, the teacher appears." Pain makes us ready and is a unique motivator. It is one of the greatest resources we have in life. It warns, reminds, and guides us. Pain also is the common denominator for what is called "the school of experience," which happens when what we were hoping for is eclipsed by something else.

This book also addresses the needs of leaders everywhere, in small and large organizations, at home and in the community, who are hungry for a concrete way of understanding and acting as a leader. The type of leadership I'll describe in this book reaches way beyond the bottom line, literally flipping their focus to build an organization that is upside down: leaders who are there to see their people succeed—knowing the money will follow. Not that profits aren't important—but when they are the primary motive for what we do at work, the passion is eclipsed by stress and the heart of the organization is replaced with a cash register. As a friend of my great-grandfather, the late H. J. Heinz once said, "The best businesses run on heart power." Capital is a by-product of inspired business leadership because inspired leadership is the catalyst for genuine, effective, lasting progress in all human endeavors. *I have seen repeatedly this type of game-changing leadership is a talent that can be developed and even mastered with commitment, coaching, self-awareness, and desire.*

On the other side of the pain, chaos, and confusion lies the potential for a business you are proud of—one that has meaning, is no longer focused on survival but on creating genuine significance, and is more profitable than you ever hoped. What's more, this business includes a team that is energized and thinks more and more like owners. This book will help you create these results because inspired leadership is the stimulus to ending the chaos and creating clarity, alignment, and results.

**So ... Who Is Bob Spiel?**

You might be saying this sounds intriguing and even hopeful ... but why should I listen to or trust what this guy has to say? Is he able to teach me about how to run my business and lead others?

Yes, I believe so. But let me tell you a little about myself, and then you can make that decision for yourself. Leadership and team building have been passions of mine since youth, and I now have a thirty-year track record in developing genuine leaders and building high-performance teams. Even before earning an MBA and leading in business, I cut my teeth with leadership as a young man, serving as student body president for one of the largest high schools in Arizona. I was also elected governor of the Arizona YMCA Model Legislature and speaker of the house for Arizona Boys State. Throughout my career, I've been known as "Mr. Team" and have had the opportunity to take on tough, turnaround situations as a hospital CEO, surgical center CEO, and also as an operations director for two Fortune 500 companies where I led teams of up to 500 people while establishing world-class systems and cultures. For over ten years I have been a coach, author, and speaker to small business owners across the country—teaching leadership and team-building principles. The results from this have been personally gratifying and energizing. But, more important, they have been transformative and profitable for my clients. It is especially exciting to see leaders and their teams experience the joy, increased productivity, decreased stress, and sense of ownership that occurs when they take a different approach to doing business—flipping their focus from top-down leadership to what I call upside-down leadership.

My path to understanding the transformational power of inspired, upside-down leadership began with my very first job after graduating from college. The position was with a large agribusiness company in northern California that had established a culture within each of its divisions that was very autonomous and entrepreneurial; each was treated like its own small business. Our divisional general manager was a brilliant businessman who was facing a tough environment of increasing costs and decreasing commodity prices—a perfect recipe for failure. There was something unique about this general manager, however. Rather than blame the situation and view everything as a problem, he was never down and consistently looked for opportunities in all the challenges he confronted. That was unlike anything I had experienced before. I soon found he had been a teaching assistant for Dr. Stephen Covey—the acclaimed business and leadership guru, and best-selling author of the *Seven Habits of Highly Effective People*—a few years before Covey left academia and started his own consulting firm. Jim Faber was the general manager's name, and he quickly became a mentor, as I was young, hungry, and teachable. Seven years before the *Seven Habits of Highly Effective People* was published, Jim had workbooks and cassette tapes about the seven habits that became part of a required course of study for all of his direct reports. In our weekly management meetings, we would teach each other principles of one of the seven habits, and he and I would frequently have formal and informal mentoring sessions. Through all this teaching and mentoring, I began to absorb these principles and they changed how I related to my job, family, and the world. Like all great leaders, Jim had a way of deeply influencing and creating other leaders around him. His belief in me was so great that I began to believe in myself, and the four years we worked together laid the foundation for what I would achieve in the years to come.

With Jim's encouragement, I pursued a master's degree in business and then returned to the same agribusiness firm. This time, I accepted a position in a different division working for a general manager who had a reputation for being a brilliant agriculturalist. What I soon found, however, was that this man (I'll call him Nick)—though indeed highly intelligent—lacked Jim's leadership strengths. Where Jim was empowering, Nick was ultra-controlling. Jim lived a balanced life, while Nick avoided the pain that can come with family life by being a workaholic. Finally, Jim was a builder while this man was a wrecker who thought nothing of firing one or two direct reports a year. I lasted sixteen months in his organization—but discovered the lesson of a lifetime. The stark difference between these two men cemented into my heart the critical importance of leadership: I saw both the wreckage that can occur when one who is in the position to lead doesn't; and the joy, growth, and success that transpires when a leader truly does.

Two short years later, I could draw on the principles Jim imprinted onto my soul as I led operational divisions for Franklin Quest (later known as Franklin Covey, which was the world's preeminent training and development company) and then PageNet (the world's largest paging network at the time with over ten million subscribers at their zenith). In each of these roles I had between 250 and 500 team members in my organization and as many as eleven direct reports. Together, we created world-class quality, cultures, and systems while experiencing enormous growth—at rates between

25 percent and 250 percent each year. In each of these roles, I carried not only the principles I had been taught by Jim but also the activities—weekly trainings for my management team on the seven habits, formally and informally mentoring each direct report, creating self-managed work teams where possible, and monthly training meetings for the entire division. Yet the true value from Jim's mentoring was the way he taught me to look at each business situation and each relationship.

My experience with both firms was short lived, lasting about three years each, because of the pressures technology placed upon their business models. Franklin began a slow decline after the advent of the PDA (personal digital assistant—one of the ancestors of today's cell phones), and PageNet began bleeding rather rapidly once digital cell phones came onto the market and dropped the price point for nationwide cell plans. Looking for a haven where technology would not take out in a year what it took a decade to create, I jumped into health care and worked in a boutique health care–centered venture capital firm, served as a small hospital CEO, and large surgical center CEO before jumping headfirst into being a small business owner as a leadership and business coach. As scary as that transition was (and not being able to pay yourself for almost nine months can be scary), today I have the privilege of working with some of the greatest small business clients from East to West Coast as well as speaking to audiences of 200 to 800. The greatest thing is it does not feel like work because I am in full alignment (finally) with my personal mission: to lift and inspire others and to be a change agent improving lives, work, and futures. Throughout my career, the vital role of inspired leadership and team building has made the difference between success and failure. Through this book, I hope to pass on those lessons to you.

**What You Are Going to Discover**

To truly gain control of your life and create the business you've always dreamed of, it's important to start with the one thing you can change—yourself. In chapter 2, we're going to explain how leadership can conquer the chaos growing businesses face and explore the connection between leadership and business success. I'll introduce the model of upside-down leadership and discuss how it can yield positive results not only in business but in your personal life as well. We will also see why organizations can't run faster than their leader—and why personal development is the catalyst for organizational success and greatness.

The first fundamental way leaders think differently will be taught in chapter 3. We'll take a closer look at the basic principles of upside-down leadership and explore how they differ from the traditional style of top-down leadership. Why some leaders are followed so willingly, and others very reluctantly, will be explained. This chapter will contrast seven deadly management sins with seven winning management skills.

To properly frame this discussion, we need to understand where personal development begins. Chapter 4 will explain where to put your mental and emotional focus as you begin this process.

As we strive for personal improvement, the gravitational pull of the past becomes very real—much like what a spaceship experiences as it seeks to leave Earth's orbit. Chapter 5 will outline how to conquer the internal demons that hold us back. We will explore why none of us can go past the boundaries of our limiting beliefs and examine how the fear of failure places artificial limitations on us. We will also discuss how changing our perception about failure can be life-changing and how leaders recognize and actively challenge their own limiting beliefs.

In chapter 6 we dive into your role as a leader, what can be delegated and what can't be delegated, and what effective delegation will do for your team. We will identify why setting the vision, direction, and pace are instinctive jobs of leaders—detailing why, what, and where the group is going. From there we'll explore how leaders delegate the work of carrying out their vision. And, critically important, we'll describe how leaders get out of the way—establishing genuine ownership and participation throughout the business.

Chapter 7 will further dissect the uniquely effective mindset of an upside-down leader. The ultimate role of a leader will be detailed as well as the consistent habits established by truly inspiring leaders. We'll look at how leaders work themselves out of a job and become Transfacilitative Leaders™.

Chapter 8 is all about how you release control and still get results. We'll outline how to shift from control to influence using clear roles, goals, and metrics. Making accountability natural and easy, as well as eliminating most conflict at work and enjoying the overall impact that clarity in an organization provides for everyone, will be identified.

In chapter 9, we'll look at how to build a truly effective team of owners. I'll explain how asking fundamental questions about what you should and shouldn't be doing will identify opportunities for ownership that are yet being developed within your organization. We'll also explore how maintaining the focus of the team as well as team members creates accountability to self and to the group.

Have you ever wondered what keeps the magic going in a high-performance organization? In chapter 10, we'll look at the keystone activity of leadership and identify the one thing you can put in motion tomorrow to immediately improve your leadership abilities.

In chapter 11 we'll explore the possibility of building something truly sustainable and how culture is a direct reflection of the primary leader's values and style. Every business has a culture and it is the key to its destiny. In this chapter, we'll explain how personal development sets the groundwork for cultural development—to establish a culture by design instead of by default.

In chapter 12 we will consider what ultimate success in all this looks like. Is there a highest form of team—and when is a team ready to achieve this? You will find where the true impact of leadership leads and how to know when you are approaching that point. It is simple to describe ... but only attainable by following the paradigms outlined in earlier chapters.

Finally, we'll close by reiterating the case for leadership, as well as a call for mentorship -- because genuine leaders always create other leaders. That desire becomes a part of their purpose in life, and nothing becomes more satisfying than seeing others ignite the flame of leadership within their own heart and soul.

Each chapter ends with what I call a "Coach's Challenge." These are questions you may choose to work through to help fully absorb and process the ideas in the chapter. In my work with clients, I frequently give such homework to help them begin to capture the lessons at a deeper level. Questions are a powerful catalyst for this type of progress, as they empower you to begin making your own connections and ask further questions. Ultimately, the purpose of self-improvement and education is not to provide answers, but to realize how to ask the questions. A dramatic shift happens in our life when we finally realize that the questions themselves are the answer. These coaching questions "prime the pump" with thoughts to begin that process, and an effective way to approach them is to slow down at the end of each chapter and answer them thoughtfully, and honestly.

I promise this will be high adventure from the beginning—and a journey that is worth every effort. So, now that you know where this will take you and the rewards for going there ... let's dive in.

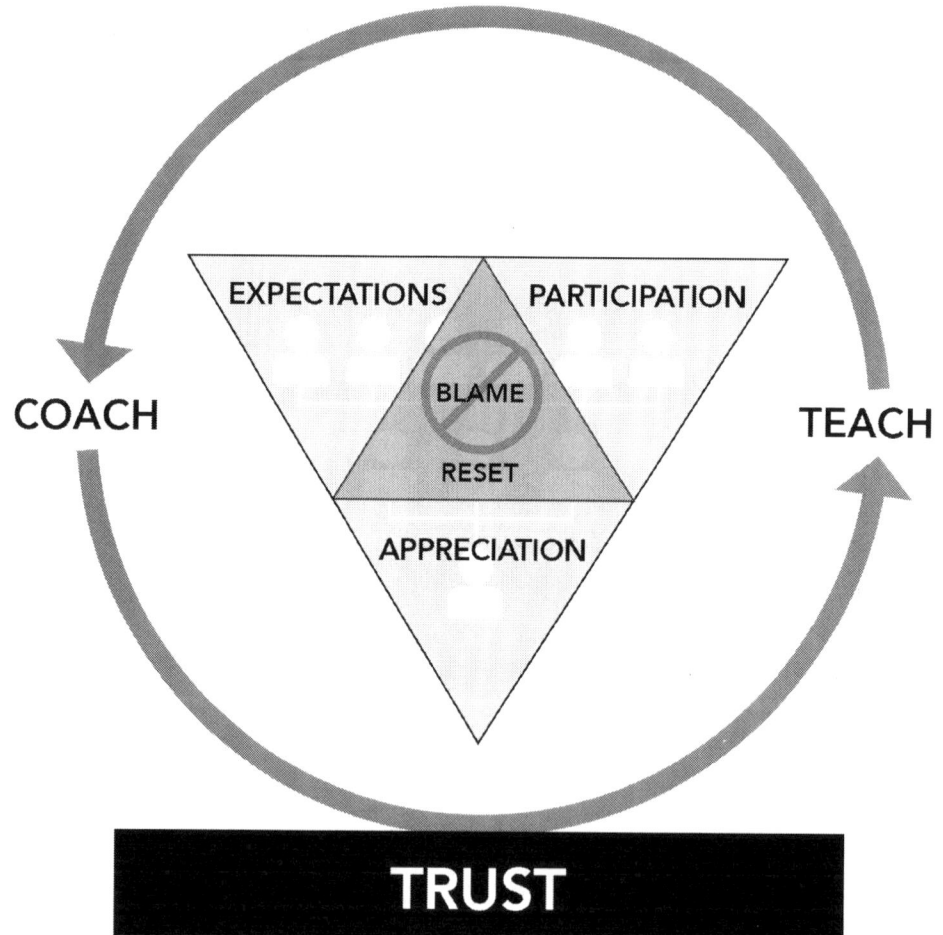

CHAPTER TWO

# Tackle Demands and Tame the Chaos by Becoming an Upside-Down Leader

*Lesson: You can't run faster than your leader.*

Day two on the job at one of the largest telecommunications firms in America, and I found myself surrounded by chaos. "Sweetheart, it's like playing football in a forest" I told my wife that night. I was standing outside at a pay phone—this was an era before cell phones, and the phone service in my temporary housing was not yet turned on. Sweat was running down my back, as the Dallas humidity held on tight on an unusually warm November evening, even at 10 p.m. After hanging up, I slowly climbed back into my car, looked into the rearview mirror, and stared into it with disbelief. What had I gotten myself into?

After only two days, the reality of the turmoil at PageNet was becoming crystal clear. The department I had been heavily recruited to lead was now working 24/7, with 350 temporary employees and a handful of PageNet managers as supervisors. All of this was happening in a poorly designed 4,500-square-foot office building—a space that was far from adequate for the growing operation. What's more, when I arrived, we were still sharing the building with 200 call center employees who were about to move into their own facility. Despite internal controls, in that setting it was anyone's guess how many pagers were walking out the door to be sold on the black market, while the pagers being shipped had to be meticulously programmed using systems that were five years old, designed for low-volume sales offices, mistake-prone, and labor intensive.

Our mission was to service the largest account ever acquired by PageNet—the billion-dollar long-distance carrier MCI. Just two months prior, the operation was ramped up to meet the growing demands coming from MCI: 500 pagers per day were being sent out, then 1,000 per day the next month, and now 2,000 per day. In the fifteen years of PageNet's history, nothing like this had happened. Previously, a strong metro sales office might place 2,000 pagers in an outstanding month. By the time I came on board, that number was being shipped consistently each day and still sales continued to climb. No one knew where it would stop.

For context, this was the 1990s—a time when landlines were everywhere, long distance was a service customers paid for heavily, and pagers were like today's cell phones. MCI thought that they had found a solution to reduce customer "churn," a phrase used to describe one of their biggest problems, when customers turned off their service and went to another long-distance carrier. They began leasing pagers to customers with MCI logos on them that were still owned and operated by PageNet. The thinking was that if an MCI customer had an MCI pager and then gave their number out to family and friends, that customer would hesitate to turn off their long-distance service—since phone numbers were not transferrable to other devices back then. They now had a hard "asset" in their hands they wouldn't want to turn off or tell friends they were no longer using.

My appointed purpose with the company was to tame the chaos, make order out of the confusion, handle the near-exponential growth while avoiding order backlogs, improve security, and prepare to take on additional accounts within the next two to three months. My background in logistics and order fulfillment at Franklin Quest had landed me this job, but it wasn't technical know-how that was needed now. What was needed was leadership. The business I came into was rife with low trust, poor tools, insufficient training, antiquated systems, poor management, and a terrible facility. And only leadership could cure those ills.

After five and a half restless hours of sleep that night, I returned to the facility for a critical meeting. In our conference room sat three highly paid Anderson (now Accenture) consultants ready to hand off their report on how we could emerge from this mess. The consultants, who had been hired months before I arrived, presented carefully constructed charts and graphs showing what was all too obvious: PageNet had grabbed a tiger by the tail and no one knew when it would stop. At Franklin, I had become used to 25–30 percent growth each year, but this was 100 percent growth each month and was still escalating. After their presentation, they looked at me and said, "Bob, we need to move into an actual distribution facility within the next three to four weeks. We also need to have the systems in place to make the pager programming process happen with one swipe of a bar code, instead of five tedious programming steps by a person. The pager programming system is under way right now, and should be finished over the next month, but what are you going to do about the facility and finding the right personnel to run it?"

I was a bit dumbfounded by their recommendations. It was a huge relief to hear a programming system was in the works that would dramatically simplify the process while increasing accuracy and security. But their recommendation to move the operation within a month could not be done. At Franklin, I had championed a similar effort and it took over a year. Upon hearing their analysis, I replied, "With all due respect, we all know it will be impossible to relocate in that time frame. We have lost our window. This is the place. Now is the time. We must do it here and it is up to us to figure out what that looks like."

Together, we made it happen—and I had the privilege of leading the effort. The existing facility was transformed, new tools were acquired, intensive trainings were conducted, and, most important, new team members and managers were brought in, while others who weren't a good fit didn't stay on. Within forty-five days of my joining PageNet, the company successfully shipped 14,000 pagers in one day. Over Thanksgiving, a conveyor was installed that went from the office building out through one regular-sized door and into a UPS truck. The manual packaging process was replaced with laser scanners and package labelers. Later, that 4,500-square-foot office building was replaced with a 60,000-square-foot distribution center, and the 14,000 pagers sold to one company were replaced by 2,000 to 4,000 pagers a day for forty companies that all required bulletproof quality. Meanwhile the team of 350 had been streamlined down to 120. The chaos ended. And when the dust settled, a very confident and professional team emerged that continued to beat all previous expectations.

## The Leadership-Business Success Connection

In times of chaos—and in times of stability—there is an unmistakable connection between leadership and business success. This is true whether we are talking about a company of 3,500, a division of 350, or a small business of five team members. When chaos abounds, leadership is the single greatest element that can successfully pull the group through to the other side. Further, with the right leadership, most chaotic situations can be altogether avoided while creating a culture that is largely self-sufficient and self-sustaining—and business thrives in such an environment.

Why is it we need leadership for business success? As human beings, whether it is by nature or nurture, we are hierarchical beings. Social structure is a part of our makeup and we expect leaders to provide fundamental guidance. First, we look to them to set the vision or direction. In my work, I have found that everything else a leader does—besides carrying out their personal highest and best purpose—can be delegated, except for vision and direction. No one else can do this. No one else can set the course, shape the direction, and create the compelling vision of where a group is going.

There is another fundamental element leaders are also wholly responsible for, whether knowingly or unknowingly, and that is setting the pace. Pace is the internal rhythm, sense of urgency, and rate that tasks are accomplished. And the pace of a group is a direct reflection of the leader's pace. Teams cannot run faster than their leader. It is impossible to do.

Acknowledging this connection between leadership and success can be a frightening truth, or it can be the most liberating thought ever for a business leader. When business owners and leaders accept responsibility for their own situation, their own development, and then decide the time is now to raise the level of their game—to create change within themselves so change will happen in their organization—something amazing takes place. Ultimately, the culture in an organization reflects the values, attitudes, and morals of the primary leader or leaders; which is why personal development is the key for organizational development because like a pebble being dropped into the pond, the ripple effect is real and profound.

**Leadership Models**

Before we dive into how to develop as a leader, let's stop and consider what type of leader you want to become. We all know there are different kinds of leaders and different models of leadership. Fads and management styles come and go, but the basic elements of how a leader approaches the job and his or her team remain steadfast and are key to the success of the organization.

*Traditional Top-Down Leadership*

Ask the average person what leadership and business look like and you'll likely hear a description of the traditional organizational pyramid. Indeed, the vast majority of American businesses resemble this top-down structure. At the pinnacle of this pyramid is the owner or leader; everyone lower than them ultimately exists to see the person at the top succeed. Leaders in this traditional organization view their role as being a boss, giving orders, issuing commands, making heads roll and things happen because no one else in the organization cares or knows as much as they do.

Operating in this structure brings a host of problems for the leader, to say nothing of the underlying employees. Chief among these problems for the business owner or CEO is the tendency to burn out. As we discussed in the introduction, being a "chief everything officer" is exhausting. When a business grows, so too do the demands and to-do list of an owner who is trying to hold fast to the reins. Often, health and family life take a backseat to work. Yet despite the efforts of the leader to create a successful business, the workplace culture becomes unstable and, frankly, sick. Morale is low, turnover high. The question that wakes these business owners up in the middle of the night is, "Isn't there another way?"

*Upside-Down Leadership*

The answer is a resounding "Yes!" And that's what this book is all about—a model of leadership that flips the focus of the traditional leadership pyramid. This model grew out of the strong mentoring relationships I have been involved in, proven theories of personal success, and my professional experience working with scores of businesses in a consulting role. Upside-down leadership allows leaders to support others in becoming their best, provide vision while setting the pace of their organizations, and create a business and life of significance—while being successful and having balanced lives! When leaders and their teams flip their frame of reference from control to abundance, from top-down leadership to upside-down leadership—with clear expectations, roles, and goals; and with the end goal to create a self-perpetuating culture of unselfish teamwork—the results are life changing, personally and professionally. Upside-down leadership is the answer to the midnight cry for help, because it transforms a business from being owner dependent to organizationally and culturally dependent. CEO then means chief empowerment officer, not chief everything officer.

**Case Study: Leaders Set the Vision, Direction, and Pace**

Dr. Stevens* learned about how he was responsible for setting the vision, direction, and pace just in time to save his practice. After I spoke at a conference in Atlanta, his office manager came up to me with panic in her eyes, leading to an in-person visit of his practice. On a rainy spring afternoon, I sat in his office staring at the wall of trophies, sports memorabilia, and journals on oral, facial, and maxillofacial surgery. His office décor told me the man I was about to meet was a sports enthusiast; I already knew he was a very skilled doctor. Yet I also knew that he needed to change some of his fundamental business practices. The persistent rain outside his window, with an occasional flash of lightning, accentuated the situation he was in. I had just spent six hours interviewing the ten members of his team, getting a clear picture of the dynamics that were causing organizational chaos. Dr. Stevens sat down at the conference table in his office, leaned back in his chair, and as a broad grin spread across his face, he looked at me and asked this searching question, "Well … am I going to make it?"

There wasn't fear in his eyes but there was definite concern. I replied, "Dr. Stevens, you'll make it—but you are not going to make it how you've done in the past. There has to be change and that change has to start with you."

His practice had become extremely successful in the seven years he owned it, with a steady stream of patients and a comfortable income, but his gregarious and challenge-oriented nature had created a workplace culture that was completely unsettled. To describe his style succinctly: his tolerance for business risk was so great, and his level of personal performance so high, he welcomed every new challenge—and then would figure out what to do with it. He was continually investing in new technology, taking on new surgeries, and ramping up volume but never setting boundaries with his referring providers, with his schedule, or with his employees. Trust in his office was at an all-time low. Burnout among a very talented team was evident; though most had been with him at least four or five years, they were so tired more than half his team was ready to quit. The managers he had put in place were only adding to the chaos instead of diminishing it. The systems were inadequate. The only thing holding the team together was their loyalty to him. It seemed like they were a team that was running a hundred miles an hour all day long in a hundred different directions—yet their tires were bald and the car was starting to vibrate apart.

**Leadership Is the Catalyst to Organizational Success and Greatness**

Dr. Stevens listened intently to my advice that change would need to start with him. He leaned across the table and asked, "How do I begin this process?" That question marked the beginning of a wonderful exchange about the true nature of leadership, the needs of his team to be led effectively with care and skill, and passing that leadership on to his team members appropriately. For more than an hour we discussed the concepts covered in this book: flipping your focus by transforming your job as a leader to see that your team succeeds , setting clear expectations , creating a culture of participation and ownership , appreciating the wins that take place, and eventually getting out of the way and letting your team soar. We also discussed personal choice and how it is within everyone's grasp to master these skills *if* they have desire, passion, humility, and commitment.

In the year we worked together, Dr. Stevens chose to make a change, and that change has created a whole new practice for him. Today, his office has a completely different feel. Chaos has been replaced with clarity in his vision, expectations, schedule, and effectiveness. His output has gone up 40 to 50 percent in the same amount of surgical time, but with a schedule that is now so efficient and streamlined the tension among his team is virtually gone. His business and clinical teams are proud of the changes they have made, and while a couple of original team members have left, his office staff is second to none.

And contrasting the stress level from the first time I visited to now—it is night and day. Where initially there were frowns and tears, now there are brilliant smiles, confidence, and clarity. Just as the rainstorm that first day gave way to brilliant sunlight, the sunlight of clarity and leadership is now shining upon his business like never before. And it all started the moment Dr. Stevens exercised the greatest personal asset we all possess—the power of choice. He realized that the future direction of his practice was strictly up to him and that if nothing changed, nothing would change. He made the choice to change and then listened intently and honed new business skills—much like he had once mastered how to perform surgery. At first, the changes felt awkward and required practice, but now those skills are ingrained within him. Whereas a year ago the joy and excitement he felt daily came from performing a complex surgery, Dr. Stevens will admit the even greater excitement he feels now when he witnesses growth in his team as they continue to increase their abilities to do more and to be more, while meeting the needs of their patients more fully.

## Case Study: Organizational Change Starts with Individual Change

Small business owners Mark and Susan Jackson experienced that same power of personal choice as they sat in my office and described the situation at their orthotics and prosthetics clinic. Despite strong competition, their business had continued to grow year after year because of their caring attention to both patients and referring doctors, but now, like Dr. Stevens, they had hit a wall. Continued success meant fifteen- and sixteen-hour days for Mark as the main clinician and ten- to twelve-hour days for Susan as the office manager and bookkeeper. The couple was burned out, stressed out, and out of fuel. Their family life was suffering from the imbalance and their marriage was beginning to fray. The question they asked me seems to be the universal question of all small business owners: "Can we make it through this? Is there another way?"

My reply was the same that I had given Dr. Stevens: "You can make it—but you are not going to get there the way you got here. It is going to require new skills, new talents, and personal change." In our first meeting, I explained the vision of flipping their focus, inverting the organization, and letting their team soar. Susan grabbed on to these concepts with full force and quickly flipped her focus. Within two months, her ten-hour days had become five-hour days, and her team members were more excited and energized than ever before. She had set them free through delegating results and giving them the freedom to figure out the methods. She put scoreboards in place so she didn't lose control—instead, self-control was shared by the entire office staff. Where her face once revealed stress and con- cern, now it displayed smiles. She was now able to spend more time with her kids at home, where she wanted to be all along, and she also experienced great joy as she saw her team members excel in their jobs once they were given permission to do so.

For Mark, the process took longer. But now three years later, he, too, enjoys these same results. He is finally home in the evenings, can step away from the office for family vacations, and can devote more of his time at work to growing the business—spending 80 percent of his workday focusing on business growth and 20 percent on working inside it. The result to the business from Mark and Susan's change? For the past year, 40 percent growth!

**Leadership Can Be Developed and Mastered—the Key Is Commitment ... and Desire**

These, and countless other similar stories, show that like all other skills, leadership can be developed and mastered—though true leaders never stop growing. Often there is a question of whether leaders are born or made. I don't agree with either option. The ability to lead is found from *within* through the process of *committing* to personal change—looking directly and honestly in the mirror and coming to the realization that whatever it has taken to get you where you are, it is not going to be enough to get where you need to be. And with this commitment comes a desire to be coached. All great athletes and performers have coaches, because they all have blind sides. The same is true for leaders. It is impossible on our own for us to see fully everything we need to see in order to continue to enjoy further success and improvement.

The coaching starts here, right now. I appreciate that this type of coaching is very personal, can be painful, and is also sacred. I take my responsibility seriously to teach you principles, practices, and paradigms that will allow you to lead your team, run your business, and live your life at a level that you may now only dream of. Those dreams must be translated into a genuine desire because when difficulties arise or old habits creep back, it is your burning desire—a vision of what is out there and what is possible, and a full-throttled commitment to that vision—that will keep you moving forward.

To repeat a phrase from the introduction, there is an old Chinese proverb that says, "When the student is ready, the teacher appears." I have seen the truth of that proverb repeatedly in the work I do as a consultant and coach. If you are ready, now is the time. Let the teaching begin.

**Coach's Challenge**

1. How have you personally experienced the connection between leadership and personal success?
2. On a scale of 1–10, what is your personal level of commitment to profound personal and organizational change over the next twelve months? What are you willing to sacrifice to achieve that?
3. In what ways may you be restricting your team of employees from reaching their full potential?
4. Are you ready to be coached? If not, what would need to change in your life to be?
5. What are you losing out on right now by continuing to do things the way you always have?

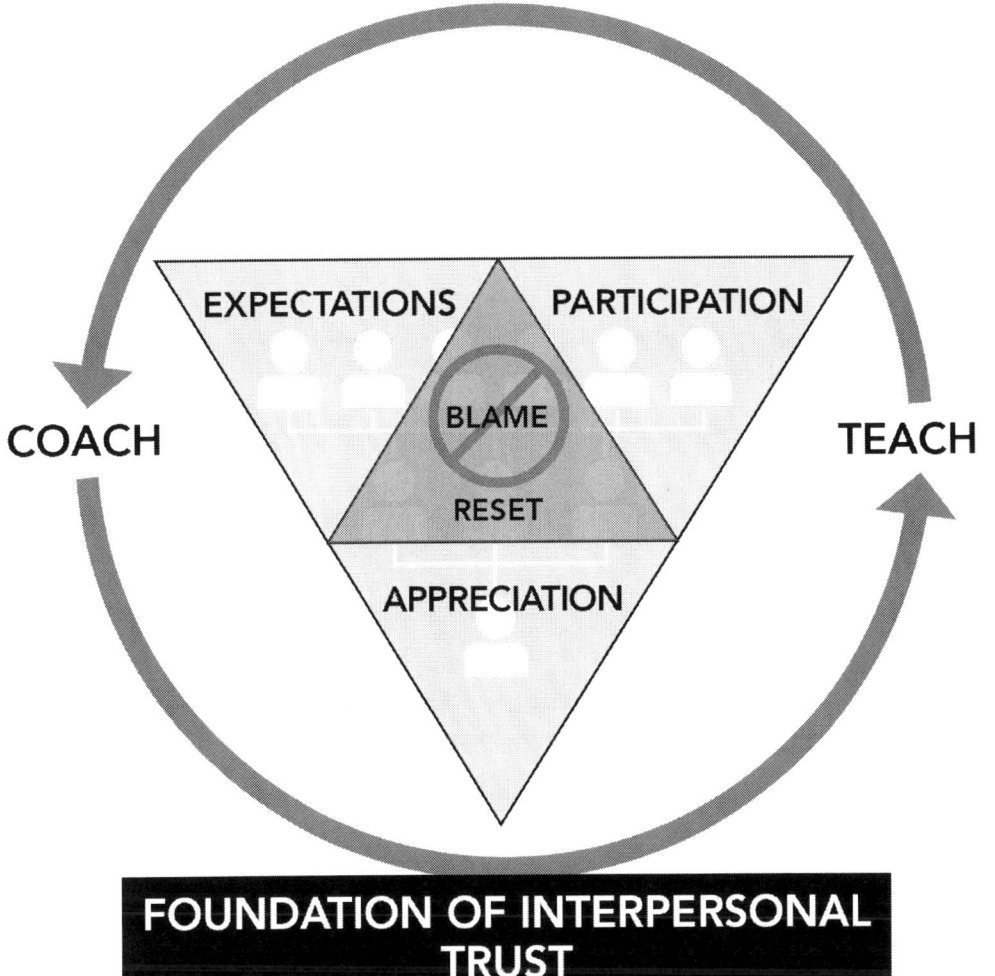

# IT BEGINS WITH TRUST:

- EXPECTATIONS
- PARTICIPATION
- BLAME
- RESET
- APPRECIATION

COACH

TEACH

**FOUNDATION OF INTERPERSONAL TRUST**

CHAPTER THREE

# Flipping Your Focus—Thinking Like an Upside-Down Leader

*Lesson: Leaders are trustworthy and care about their teams.*

We are now going to have a very frank conversation on what it takes to create a personal breakthrough and flip your focus to become an upside-down leader. This, above all, requires a different way of thinking as well as a different way of behaving and inspiring others. It may be uncomfortable at first. After all, thinking and behavior patterns become deeply ingrained with time. Yet, with practice and commitment, you can master the skills needed to lead in this way—and reap the immense and life-changing rewards that come with flipping your focus.

Let's begin by pondering the traditional top-down leadership model again to get a better understanding of why this way of leading ultimately hinders your ability to succeed. The picture we're about to paint may sound a bit too familiar. That's okay. Remember, if nothing changes, nothing changes—and a truthful look in the mirror can be one of the most life-altering actions we ever take.

Visually, this mode of leadership resembles a pyramid with Mr. or Mrs. Big at the top. Everyone in the organization exists to see that Mr. or Mrs. Big succeeds. The top-down leadership model often employs variations of what I call "the seven deadly sins of management." These common tools are often used to try to maintain control, but they demotivate teams in seven easy steps.

**Seven Deadly Management Sins**

1. *Issuing threats and ultimatums.* Fear is a poor manager's go-to emotion. It feels justified in the moment, but like crash dieting, it backfires in the long run and only makes things worse. Fear freezes negative behavior in place, stunts growth, creates poor quality, raises costs, and demoralizes teams.

2. *Comparing employees to prior team members.* Nothing destroys confidence faster (other than management sin 1) than comparing the present team member to a prior one. It is like comparing our children or discussing wages. It never yields anything positive, and only leaves others feeling bad about themselves.

3. *Consistently being inconsistent.* Never sticking to a decision creates doubt and uncertainty. It puts team members on edge and hinders their ability to perform, for fear the rules tomorrow will be different than today. If the rules in football changed constantly—during a game—how confident and motivated would teams be? Uncertainty drives team members crazy.

4. *Not backing their team.* A manager who won't fight for his or her employees loses their trust. Throwing team members under the bus to please an out-of-bounds customer tells them they are walking on ice that may crash through at any moment—it's just a matter of time.

5. *Micromanaging and not prioritizing.* Leaders who are control freaks disempower their teams, while not having priorities confuses them as to what is most important now. Both of these management sins result in employees who wait to be told what to do, while any self-motivated team members check out and leave.

6. *Breaking confidences and creating "drama triangles."* Pitting one employee against another is a frequent source of chaos in a

business. Managers do this by violating confidences, gossiping to other employees, and having a group scapegoat to divert attention away from the real problems of the business.

7. ***Being chronically negative.*** What we pay attention to grows. If all managers do is find fault and complain, they will consistently have more to complain about. The culture becomes chronically negative and goes into a downward spiral. Turnover abounds and joy is dissolved.

Ultimately, control oriented, top-down leadership has a short-term focus and disempowers team members. Leading and managing others in this way is ineffective, self-defeating, and sadly pervasive. However, many of these leaders simply do not realize there is another way. They feel stuck in a trap; leadership is all about them because of their struggling self-esteem, fear, strong ego, or other forms of fragile emotional intelligence.

**Leadership Alignment and Results**

These seven deadly sins remind me of a quote from Arthur R. Jones : "All organizations are perfectly aligned to get the results they get." Paraphrasing this slightly, I believe *leaders are perfectly aligned to get the results they get*. And what type of results has top-down leadership created in America today? The statistics are daunting: 70 percent of employees will admit they are not engaged at work, while a staggering 17 percent are actively *disengaged* and regularly sabotaging productive work. When success is all about the person at the top, here's what happens: those employees who want to contribute their highest and best will check out of the organization, and most of those who don't leave have already quit their jobs—they just stick around to collect a paycheck.

### Flip Your Thinking—and Change Your World

Those are the results of the traditional top-down organization. The great news is there's another way. And what it takes is to flip your focus and way of thinking about leadership. Just take that traditional organizational pyramid and flip it over in your mind, and then don't let it move. This is how upside-down leaders think: differently. Rather than everybody existing to see that the person at the top succeeds, in an upside-down organization, the leader or leadership team exists to see everybody in the organization succeeds.

### Shifting from Traditional Leadership to Upside-Down Leadership

What does it look like to flip your focus from a traditional leadership perspective to a model of upside-down leadership? The changes are dramatic:

- From boss to coach
- From fear to freedom
- From survival to success and significance
- From scarcity to abundance
- From chaos and confusion to clear expectations and accountability
- From perfection to excellence
- From a culture of control to a culture of participation and ownership
- From director to facilitator
- From individual employees to team members

These leaders have a long-term focus and strive to empower their team, knowing true empowerment produces what might otherwise be called miracles. They are committed to surrounding themselves with the very best and brightest talent, knowing their job is not to have all the answers ... but to know how to facilitate and pull the answers out of their team. They lead from a standpoint of hope, not fear. The seven deadly sins are clearly on their "to-don't list." In fact, they do the opposite, working to help everyone in their organization do their best and be their best. Their list of seven winning management skills might look like this to-do list:

1. Coach with hope.
2. Believe in each person
3. Be measured and consistent.
4. Support my team.
5. Empower and prioritize.
6. Create a culture of trust, responsibility, and accountability.
7. Find the best in people and situations.

As a leader or owner accepts this mindset, and leaves the top-down culture forever in the dust, the success that takes root and then occurs within their organization is exponentially greater than in a traditional organization.

Upside-down leaders look at business from an entirely different perspective. Of course, they are running a business and are aware of the bottom line, but that doesn't drive their every action. Rather, achieving their bottom line is the result of consistently doing the right things. Indeed, they have a more organic approach—focusing not only on operations but on the people who work for them—and that flipped focus naturally leads to, and even surpasses, their desired outcomes. They embody what Zig Ziglar once said: "You don't build a business. You build people, and then people build your business."

**The Lesson of a Lifetime**

I first was introduced to the elements and thinking of what I now call upside-down leadership from my boss, friend and mentor, Jim Faber, on a sunny, spring afternoon in northern California. The air was soft as the trees were just starting to open and welcome the warmth with their new leaves. A beautiful column of light was streaming through his office window. As I settled into one of the two chairs in his office opposite his desk, he looked at me and asked me one of the most profound questions of my life: *"Bob would you like to know what your agenda is as a business leader?"*

Jim knew that I was a hungry and eager student, and I quickly replied, "Of course, Jim. I'd love to know what my mission is." Leaning back in his old chair, he smiled before beginning, "Well, it's four things."

"You're kidding me ... four things?" I said. Moving forward in his chair, putting his elbows on the desk, and leaning in, he said, "Yes, four things and if you do these well, you'll succeed."

"I'm all ears," was my quick but hesitating response. (Inside my thoughts were bouncing around: "Really? Four things? C'mon. There's got to be a catch." But I soon found he meant what he said.)

Holding one finger in the air, he stated, "First and foremost, you must create an environment of trust. Trust is the foundation of all human relationships. When you have it, you have magic; when you don't, you are building on sand. Nothing can replace the essential element of trust." I got this point readily. Jim was the supreme example of a leader who fostered trust. He was honest, straightforward, didn't play favorites. In addition, he was non-political, a problem solver, and extremely good at his job. Stephen Covey described trust between people as being a function of both character and competence. Jim had both.

I was still digesting the first point when Jim jumped into the second..."Next, as a leader you must clarify expectations. Clarify them first for yourself and then for your team. The goal is to ensure it is crystal clear in all hearts and minds where you are going, and why, and how you are going to get there. Without clear expectations, how do you know where you are going as an organization and how everyone's role contributes to that end goal?" As with point one, he was an excellent role model for point two. He empowered his team by making it clear what the endpoint was and how each of our contributions mattered. He was an expert at painting a picture of an outcome and then pulling out from all of us how we were going to make that happen—while then holding us accountable to those outcomes.

I sat there pondering these first two points, seeing how he had internalized them so well, when he quickly held up three fingers and said, "Third, get the needed tools. Provide the leadership to get the training, the technology, and the equipment needed to give your people the tools to succeed." He added, "The best indication of knowing a tool is perfectly suited is that it makes work easier, more efficient, cheaper, and even more fun." Check number three now went off in my brain. I knew that under Jim's leadership, the company had acquired several new and innovative tools, and let go of some old and outdated ones.

I began absorbing these three keys to success, seeing for the first time that the role of a leader is in so many ways that of a catalyst—providing the missing ingredient that makes progress happen. He had modeled these qualities repeatedly in his role as general manager of this business division. Jim walked his talk. He created trusting relationships all around him because he was trustworthy. He established clear expectations and had a clear vision. I knew he was going to lead this organization, come what may, through whatever economic turmoil may be ahead and find solutions that would permit us to be the last man standing. He was going to reduce cost, improve quality, improve output, right-size our personnel, and make it an open and transparent organization. His pace was steady and fast—yet measured. He didn't believe in wasting time, motion, or effort. He fought to get the tools that we needed and he would continually clarify expectations.

Reflecting on the Jim Faber I had grown to know and admire, he then placed the capstone on his four-part recipe to success. With confidence that came from experience and success, and a huge smile on his face, he leaned back and said, "And with these three things firmly in place ... you get out of the way." He let that punch land, those words hitting me like a thunderbolt. "Get out of the way." The message was clear—that's what it means to be a leader. With the three foundational elements of trust, targets, and tools in place, your goal is clear. It is to build an organization that is so powerful, so well tuned, so intentional that your purpose as the group's leader then becomes one of expanding the organization's capabilities and boundaries, finding new and better tools, developing new and better markets, mining additional opportunities or ways to refine what you have today while your team owns what happens *within* the preset boundaries of the organization.

He wrapped up the conversation by clearly framing the mindset of this upside-down leader: "View your job as working yourself out of a job. Think of your role in an entirely different light. If your job is to work yourself out of a job, how do you approach each day? How do you approach training and delegating? What gets you up in the morning? *How does that one thought change everything?* In one profound way. As a leader, it is not about me—it's all about those I lead. My job is to expect their best, and then do all in my power to help them do their best."

## Where Am I Now?
## Leadership Self-Assessment

A business is a very accurate mirror for a leader. My years in business have shown me that we create around us what is inside us.

Evaluate the culture of your business. Between the two choices below, circle the one that best describes what you see going on today. Be totally honest.

- Contention or collaboration?
- Finger-pointing or accountability?
- Burnout or fun?
- Fear or hope?
- Scarcity or abundance?
- Entitlement or empowerment?

If you circled three or more words on the left, don't get discouraged. You are in good company—most business cultures look and feel like this, and this book will be your launching pad for an entirely new way of leading effectively. If you circled three or more on the right, you are already on the path of an upside-down leader. Keep reading to discover more, because it will only help you further clarify your role as a leader and your ultimate goal.

## Becoming a Leader Others Will Follow "Down a Badger Hole"

### *The Level Five Leader*

To provide greater perspective on this type of leadership, I'd like to introduce you to Jim Collins's legendary book *Good to Great* and to what he calls a "Level Five Leader." Among all the characteristics his research concluded from companies who bested their competitors in terms of multiples of growth over an entire decade, the first characteristic he named was a phrase his book coined called "Level Five Leadership." He doesn't say it using my verbiage ... but Level Five Leaders are genuine upside-down leaders. They are individuals who, rather than desiring the spotlight be placed on them, view their role as a catalyst. They ask the right questions, consistently hire the right people and place them in the right roles, maintain the right focus, set the right pace, create the correct vision and frame of reference, *and then get out of the way.* From there they work on the boundaries of the organization—doing their highest and best, while "their people" are engaged in their highest and best as well.

One noteworthy point from Collins's book was that Level Five Leaders are rarely heard of. They are individuals with a fierce will to win, but low ego and developed emotional intelligence. They are certainly results oriented, yet wise in the ways of getting things done. And ultimately, they understand that champions compete only against themselves.

Once you come across a Level Five Leader, you never forget it. Jim Faber was one. So was a leader I had the opportunity of working with for two years, one of the founders of Franklin Quest (now Franklin Covey): Dennis Webb. Dennis was the exact opposite of a top-down leader. He had a way of inspiring everyone around him to strive to do more than they ever thought possible, while his entire viewpoint was, "How can I help my people succeed?"

One day in a management meeting, he shared his personal "check-in" philosophy to see if he was succeeding at leading his team. He looked for four things:

1. When walking in the halls or otherwise passing people, do they look me in the eye or do they look down? If they look down, there's low trust—they are afraid of me.
2. In meetings, do my management team members have the courage to disagree with me? If they don't, that's a problem. That means they are afraid of me also.
3. Do we experience a lot of turnover? If so, what does that tell me? What does that say about what we are doing right or what we are doing wrong?
4. What do the numbers tell me? Numbers tell stories; what are the stories?

Dennis was a dynamic individual, not because of a natural magnetism, but because he walked his talk, loved what he did, inspired greatness in others, and conveyed to his team how much he cared. While he was very clear and intentional about where he was going (he had to as one of the founders of a public company), he also knew he wasn't going to get there alone. You could see in his eyes, and from his actions, that he felt his role as a leader was to build those around him so that they could essentially do his job. In the days I worked with him, a colleague framed his leadership abilities perfectly: "I would follow him down a badger hole." And she wasn't alone in those sentiments. Everyone who worked for Dennis Webb felt the very same way. The trust he cultivated in his team was so strong, and our belief in his intentions so high, it didn't matter what the mess was we would find ourselves in. With Dennis Webb at the helm we would come out on top ... together. This is the type of leader we can all aspire to become.

**The People We Trust to Lead Us**

Why did Dennis Webb's entire team feel that way? In fact, why do we as people follow some so willingly, giving them all our loyalty and trust and heart, but follow others so reluctantly? Frequently in my seminars, I ask the audience to take part in a little exercise. I hang up two blank banners in the room and hand out pads of Post-it Notes. First, I ask them to jot down the characteristics of outstanding leaders they have experienced or known. Next, I ask them to list some of the characteristics of weak or ineffective leaders they have experienced or known. For each of those questions, they are given ninety seconds to work as a group of four to six. Once the Post-it Notes are attached to the banners, two volunteers are asked to review the notes for a minute or two and then come back to the front of the room with summaries.

What is fascinating about these two questions? Whether the seminar is in Atlanta, Portland, DC, Omaha, or Adelaide, Australia, the answers that come back are consistently the same: we follow individuals who create environments of high trust, who are honest, clear about where they are going, and who truly care about the people who are on their teams and in their organizations. And we don't follow leaders who are angry, arrogant, critical, disrespectful, lazy, mean, and selfish (like the seven deadly sins alludes to). Repeatedly, I am reminded in this exercise that we instinctively know who we will follow. Indeed, our knowledge of whom we should place our trust in and be mentored and taught by, and whom we shouldn't, seems hardwired . The phrase that comes up repeatedly to summarize why some leaders are so readily followed is: they care. They care. Amazing it can be that simple.

**Leaders Who CARE**

*I Believe in Who You Are*

Through the work I have done with leaders, it has dawned on me there are two types of care that must be employed by every upside-down leader. The first care is shown through a habit of courtesy, appreciation, respect, and encouragement (CARE). It's a care that is centered on the intrinsic worth of each team member. It conveys the message that I believe in who you are. It's the belief Jim Faber fostered in his management team, and Dennis Webb created through the way he empowered others.

This belief is critical for both leaders and their teams. Covey once described leadership as believing so fully in others that they finally begin to believe in themselves. It is the true definition of a coach. A genuine coach is so committed to the growth and success of those within their stewardship, it is obvious that it's their mindset.

*I Believe in Who You Can Be*

Along with believing in who they are, there is another critical—and perhaps even more important—state of mind an upside-down leader must have: I believe in who you can be. So along with the habits outlined above of courtesy, appreciation, respect, and encouragement, an upside-down leader also challenges, is skilled at holding others accountable, and willing to set requirements and educate, educate, educate.

Together, these two mindsets create a potent force and cause others to instinctively give their heart and soul, their dedication and commitment, their very best work and very best thought to that type of leader.

The first time I encountered someone who led in this way, I was not yet working in a business setting. I was still in high school. My senior year, I had the privilege and opportunity to serve in the student council as class president and student body president. My high school in Mesa Arizona, Westwood High School, was at that time one of the largest and most acclaimed high schools in the state. And it had a culture where the student council worked on issues and projects that mattered to the student body.

At Westwood, we had a competition between the sophomore, junior, and senior classes. The winning class would receive the coveted class-of-the-year award at the end-of-year school assembly. We competed with floats, with plays that were written by classmates, with whacky track meets and whacky swim competitions, with fundraising for international student exchange, for decorating the school for Christmas time and even our spirit in the very first spirit rally of the year. With all this going on ... it was a lot of work to be in student council.

I remember finishing up work on a homecoming float at 4:00 in the morning the day of homecoming and routinely staying up till midnight for two weeks getting Christmas decorations ready to put up in our building. What inspired a bunch of high school kids to do this was not only the sense of competition, class loyalty, and pride. No, the drive came from something much deeper than that. We were inspired by our student council advisor, a very wise and remarkable leader named Neil Merrill. Like Dennis Webb, he knew where he was going but he had very low ego. Yes, he was a spirited and energetic man, but when he looked you in the eye, when he talked to you about your project, when we met with him and convened our group of student council members together, you instantly knew two things about Neil Merrill: how much he believed in you and how much he believed in who you could be. We all felt it and we responded to that type of leadership.

**The Path of Personal Leadership**

In the opening two chapters, we have spent a lot of time talking about you and your mindset as a leader, how change starts with you, and how you need to eliminate certain thoughts to initiate that desired change. In the chapters that follow, we'll take a closer look at those thought processes. The first is to stop the blame game. Blaming and victimizing limit our ability to solve problems, decrease our personal creative power, and back us into a corner.

The next step is to establish the ability to hit the reset button, to let go of the past, and challenge your limiting beliefs. There are a host of limiting beliefs we all bring to the table. As we go about life, we pick them up along the way—some as a youth, others as an adult. They are all based upon experience and they all set the boundaries of what we believe is possible. The limiting belief of perfection instead of excellence is pervasive, destructive, and a false paradigm. Leaders must gain the ability to actively challenge their limiting beliefs by recognizing them and then piercing through them.

The next step is to realize your job as a leader is to delegate everything except vision, pace, and direction. You know you are succeeding in this role when your desk and your calendar include only the things that you alone can do. Everyone else in the organization is also doing their highest and best in the things they can do, and they are perfectly aligned with their sense of personal and organizational mission.

Finally, with these principles as the foundation, the whole paradigm of leading upside down is the final step of personal leadership change: growing your organization's capabilities, bringing in new tools, creating new opportunities, doing only what you can do while allowing your team to do the rest. Upside-down leaders understand that the people around them are their greatest asset–and that delegating tasks and responsibilities to the right people expands the leader's capability exponentially. That is the path that flipping your focus will put you on. That is the path to true personal and professional success.

**Coach's Challenge**

1. Looking back on your career, have you committed any of the seven deadly sins of management? If so, how did they work in the long run?
2. What about the seven winning management skills? How do you currently measure up when it comes to possessing these skills? Which of these might require more of your focus and energy?
3. Review the questions Dennis Webb asked himself to gauge the trust within his business. How would you answer those for your organization and the teams you lead?
4. Grade yourself in your present practices of showing courtesy, appreciation, respect, and encouragement (CARE)? For any grade that's not an A, what can you do to make it an A?
5. How do you feel about the goal of working yourself out of your job and not digging yourself deeper into it? What possibilities does that thought open up to you? What fears does it raise? How could this change your business and your life?
6. What more can you do to build leaders around you and pass on the wisdom you've gained through personal experience?
7. Think about the great leaders you have experienced in your life. Why did you follow them? What lessons are there for you in their example that showed they used both kinds of CARE?

# THE HEART OF UPSIDE DOWN LEADERSHIP:

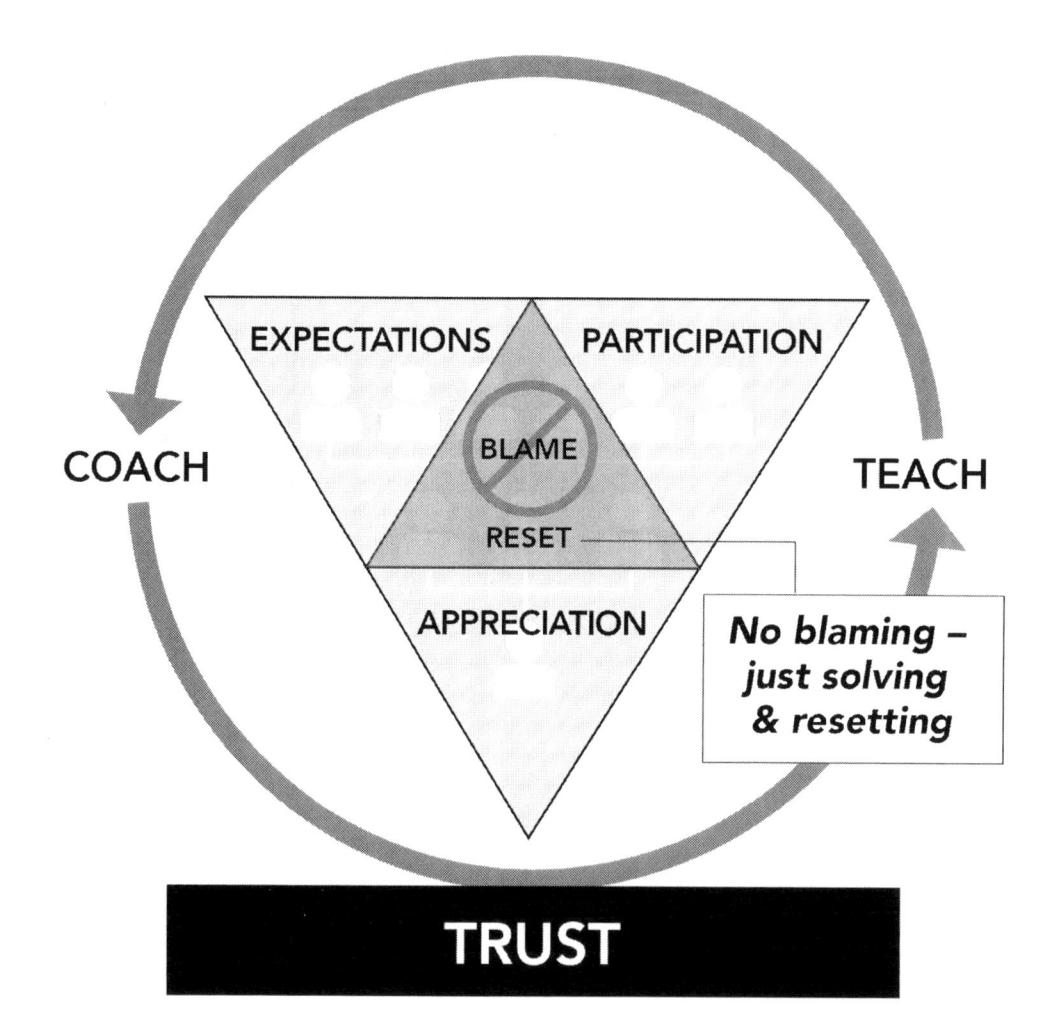

- EXPECTATIONS
- PARTICIPATION
- BLAME
- RESET
- APPRECIATION

COACH

TEACH

*No blaming – just solving & resetting*

**TRUST**

CHAPTER FOUR

# Upside-Down Leaders Cast Aside Blame and Take Personal Responsibility

*Lesson: Leaders do not blame. Leaders solve.*

On a crisp spring morning, south of Portland, Oregon, as the clouds from the Pacific were rolling through the Willamette Valley, a group of scouts and their leaders were splitting wood for a service project. The wood splitter had been rented from a local hardware store and the melodic sound of the motor, combined with the hard thump of the piston splitting the wood, became a small symphony in the forest. The smell of pine filled the air. Then this ambience all changed in a flash. Dr. John White, the group's Scoutmaster, was the one standing closest to the wood splitter and he sensed a profound pain in his left hand. Looking down he yelled, "Turn off the machine, boys. I just cut off my thumb!"

All who were there when the accident occurred could not figure out how it happened. Nobody remembers his hand being in the wrong location, but the evidence was clear because from the knuckle up, his left thumb had been severed. Racing to the hospital with only a portion of Dr. White's thumb still attached to his hand, this small group arrived at the emergency room knowing full well this could end his career. Dentists need two hands to be able to perform their work with patients. After being quickly triaged, he saw the attending physician, who soon delivered the worst news possible: the only thing they could do was remove his thumb. The cut was too rough for it to be reattached.

In that moment, John White had a decision to make. How would he react to what happened? Where would he put his focus? Anyone can see how easy it would be to sink into despair and wallow in self-pity upon receiving such news. But Dr. White was a true leader and knew that blaming would get him nowhere. So rather than stopping to cast fault on himself or the machine, or even the fact that he was on the outing, he immediately shouldered the responsibility for what took place and asked, "Who else is there who can help me?" "Where else can I go?" "How much time do I have to get this thumb reattached?" Rather than fall into a victim mindset centering on "Why this? Why me?" Dr. White sought a solution asking the more profound questions of "Who can help? How can this be turned around?" Those questions made all the difference, as calls went out to other hospitals in the area. A skilled hand surgeon was located an hour away and a successful surgery took place with a better than 50 percent chance the thumb would heal completely with proper home care and some luck.

The next challenge White faced had to do with his practice. He would not be able to see patients for at least three months. And just as the loss of a thumb can end a career for a dentist, the loss of a dentist to a practice for that length of time can be devastating. Once again, he could have let a victim mindset take hold of him. Instead, White and his team immediately went to work to find other dentists in his community who could fill in for him. From his hospital room, he began calling retired dentists in his area. Backups were found for the short term, while other doctors who could make a longer commitment were also sought. He also met with his employees right after being discharged and created very specific plans to allow the team to ride through the storm and emerge from it better and stronger. Tragedy has a way of revealing a person's core, whether strengths or weaknesses, and it does the same for a team. With complete faith in each other, and loyalty to Dr. White, the team members worked their plan and the practice continued. White trusted his team, didn't micromanage the process, and enjoyed the undivided time he had with his family during the recovery period, even taking his oldest son to Philadelphia for a science contest the last week before he returned to work. The thumb he fought so hard to protect healed completely, and while it no longer bends, it works perfectly for him. Within the first week of returning to work, he was as busy as he had been just before the accident. His positive can-do attitude created a miracle.

## Upside-Down Leaders Think Differently: They Do Not Blame—They Solve

Life is full of challenges big and small, and the choice presented to each of us is clear: In any one of the difficulties from life or business that is brought to us, we can play the Owner Card or the Victim Card. And upside-down leaders fight the feeling of victimhood like a cancer. They realize that being a victim shuts down all possibilities for the future, limits their personal power, and sets them up for failure. They make it part of their character to habitually flip their internal focus, so that instead of taking the victim stance and asking the dead-end questions of "Why this? Why me?" they consistently ask "What can I do? How can this be solved? And What lessons are there in this?" The dictionary separates the definitions of "victim" and "victor" by only five words, but in our lives the separation must be light-years apart. Victimhood has no place in a leader's heart—or in the hearts of those he or she leads. Adopting this position is the starting place of personal leadership ... and the starting place on the road to personal and group victory.

### *Blaming Is a Dead End*

A non-business example illustrates this truth succinctly by contrasting the thought processes of two high school football coaches. In sharing this story, you might think I am a sports junkie, and truthfully I'm not. But this is something I personally witnessed at my kids' high school in our hometown of Idaho Falls, Idaho. It is the clearest example of how blaming is a dead end, while shouldering personal responsibility is the beginning of greatness.

Over three consecutive seasons, the varsity football team for the Hillcrest Knights played twenty-seven games without a single victory. Their performance became so poor that when the team made a first down, you might have thought they made a touchdown, and a touchdown sounded in the stands like they had won the game. In his last season as head coach, a man I will call Coach Smith led them to a heartbreaking record of defeat, where they scored just thirty-four points while their opponents scored over three hundred. The student body that once showed up to every game stopped attending. The only people left in the stands were brokenhearted parents and grandparents, hoping their boys could handle one more loss.

Our youngest son, Paul, played for Coach Smith for two seasons; in his senior year, he left the program to run cross-country and be part of a winning team. Had he stayed on the football team, he would have been with the rest of the team who heard Smith's tragic and telling end-of-season locker room speech. In that final "pep talk," while the team had the reality of another loss staring them in the face, Smith screamed at the boys. He called them a bunch of losers, said they would never amount to anything, and declared that they had no skill or talent. In short, he was saying, "This is all your fault. If you only listened to me, the outcome would be different. I am putting all the blame on you. I have no part of this."

Shortly after this explosion, Coach Smith was relieved of his position, and the rest of the coaching staff quit as well. This group had completely bought into the idea that the boys alone were responsible for the horrible record and it had nothing to do with them. Blaming was rampant.

### *We Have a Choice to Own or Blame, and to Hit Reset or Rewind*

Within a few months, a new coach was recruited out of California to lead this football team. His name was Darin Owens, and his approach to coaching was notably different. Unlike most high school football coaches who you can quickly identify from the stands, this man did not easily stand out to fans. There was no yelling, pacing, or clipboard throwing. The first time I watched a game, I couldn't tell who the coach was, but the boys knew, and he was in their every movement, heart, and mind. And with Darin Owens as head coach, the very next year this identical group of young men (minus a few graduating seniors) who had lost twenty-seven games in a row, compiled an impressive 10–1 record, won the Idaho 4A state championship, and broke three state records in the process. Notably, this was the third program Coach Owens had turned around in his career.

What created such an incredible about-face for this team? First and foremost, in stark contrast to Coach Smith, blaming was not in Darin Owens' vocabulary. Personal responsibility was shouldered from his position as head coach, through the assistant coaches, and then to each team member. When a mistake was made in practice, rather than grind the mistake in a player's face the way Smith did, Owens would approach the player and ask if he knew what he had just done. They would discuss it and then resume play. As the preseason started, he had an unusual style of creating personal responsibility. Each player would set daily personal practice goals, write them on an index card, and then tape them to his locker. If the goals were met, a new card was placed on the locker. If not, the old and new cards were placed side by side until goals were met. And unlike other head coaches who hover over everything, because he was also the offensive coach, when the defense was practicing he would be meeting with the other offensive coaches off the field.

His entire style was about moving forward, taking personal responsibility, and allowing individual players to own their results. In his first team meeting with the players after accepting the position, Coach Owens could see that most of them had checked out. Every player was wondering what this new coach could do for them that the other coach couldn't. The boys were also stuck in a deep pattern of blaming. Sensing their despair, Owens asked the group of boys to stand on their feet and then take a long, hard look over their left shoulder. He held them there for 15 to 20 seconds, and then he asked them to take a long, hard look over their right shoulder. Finally, he instructed them to look at him. He then said these very important words: "Gentlemen, that is the last time you are ever looking back on Hillcrest football. From now on, you are only looking forward."

Owens knew that in life we fundamentally have two choices: we can either hit the reset button or the rewind button. We can either focus on the past and get stuck in a pattern of blaming—and the example of Coach Smith shows it is a dead end—or we can push reset and focus on solving the problem head-on. This is true in every human endeavor, whether we are talking about football, parenting, owning a business, or leading a nonprofit. There is one litmus test that I have found to determine if someone thinks like a leader: Do they blame or do they solve? *Leaders do not blame. Leaders solve.* Let me repeat that: leaders do not blame; leaders solve. If you want to know if somebody thinks like a leader, listen to that person's dialogue. Leaders are not victims. Leaders are not gossipers. Leaders accept personal responsibility and *then* shoulder that responsibility by seeking solutions. And like Darin Owens, they spread that ownership and responsibility throughout their organization.

**Moving from Scapegoats to Solutions**

Is this an easy place to get to? No—and it is not intended to be. The world we live in seems to spend an inordinate amount of time searching for scapegoats. We see it in politics, the media, the business world, and even among entire societies. Money is made, power is gained, and control is reinforced through victimization. Escaping into the world of blame seeks to insulate us from the reality of the situations we have got ourselves into. But, as I have said before, blaming is a dead end.

Sometime during seminars, I ask participants to list as many frustrations as they can in a minute and a half. These frustrations, however, must be full statements like "I can't lose weight" or "My husband won't listen to me." In just ninety seconds, some attendees come up with as many as twelve to fifteen frustrations. These are people, things, or circumstances that, they believe, are all affecting their happiness.

Participants are then challenged to pick just one of their frustrations and write for a minute and a half on how they can solve that problem. I suggest they begin by simply asking themselves, "What can I do to solve this?" For many, answering this question is a deeply personal experience. They find solutions they had never thought of before. For others, the exercise is just another source of frustration because their mindset has become so fixed with the habit of placing blame on others. To them it seems safer to focus on the blame because it shields themselves from guilt and pain.

But those who make the conscious choice to flip their focus from finding scapegoats to finding solutions quickly separate themselves from the crowd and enter on to the path of significance. Ending the blame game is the start of personal leadership because we only become RESPONSE-ABLE for our life and future by being RESPONSIBLE. How can such a simple discovery prompt such a move? Because taking ownership makes things happen like nothing else.

Persistent, proactive, personal responsibility effects change within us, and that change begins to transform our world.

This letting go of blame is, most often, a deeply felt moment of truth that stirs within us, as the psychologist and holocaust survivor Victor Frankl wrote in his book Man's Search for Meaning, "the last of the human freedoms—to choose one's attitude in any given set of circumstances; to choose one's own way." For the Hillcrest Knights football team, that moment was standing there with Darin Owens leading them. For me, it was the first time reading these words by Stephen Covey: "The way we think about a problem IS the prob-lem." For each of us, if we allow the pain of life to be a catalyst for humility, there can come a moment when we stand face-to-face with ourselves, accept responsibility for where we are, and decide it's time for change; it's time to stop believing everyone else is to blame that we aren't where we want to be, and it's now up to me. That is when we come to ourselves, and leadership is born.

**Coach's Challenge**

1. How can you fight the feelings of being a victim?
2. Has blaming become habitual to you—and if so, can you see how it is limiting your progress?
3. Will you stop blaming others for your lack of accomplishment and look within yourself to recognize your own faults and weaknesses to turn yourself into a genuine leader?
4. Think of a great leader who has influenced your personal life. What kind of attributes does this person have?
5. What will you do to start developing, or continue developing, these leadership attributes that will benefit your life and your business?

CHAPTER FIVE

# Let Go of the Past and Challenge Your Limiting Beliefs

*Lesson: Leaders refuse to let yesterday hold tomorrow hostage.*

Standing on the deck of a sailing ship as the fog began to form was unlike anything I had experienced growing up in the desert of Arizona. Little did I know what was about to happen next.

One month after graduating from high school, I found myself 3,000 miles from home saying "Sir, yes sir!" constantly, doing push-ups at the drop of a hat, marching in formation, eating and walking in a "braced" position—with a buzzed head and in the uniform of a Coast Guard Academy cadet. For my first year of college, I attended the United States Coast Guard Academy in New London, Connecticut. It was a grueling experience they call "swab year." And as a part of the initial summer of training, each freshman class spends a week sailing off the coast of Long Island on board the Coast Guard *Barque Eagle*, a tall-masted ship the United States procured from Hitler's Germany as a "spoil of war."

Early one humid summer morning in our weeklong "cruise," we were sailing off the northernmost tip of Long Island. Fog was beginning to build on the Atlantic Ocean as the rising sun affected the dew point. The ship creaked as it pushed through the waters at a comfortable speed of 14 knots. On this morning, my assigned duty was to keep the ship's log for the officer of the deck (OOD).

It was around 6:00 in the morning when, as can happen in the Atlantic, the fog that was forming suddenly enshrouded the entire ship that went on for miles. We quickly stopped our movement in the water by dropping our sails, when almost simultaneously, the officer of the deck ordered fog signals to be sounded. For those who aren't familiar with them, fog signals are a very deep bellowing sound emanating from a foghorn above the deck of a ship. They start with a very deep bass and then become even deeper and go for three seconds or so. Their sound can be heard for over a mile and is said to be loud enough to almost wake the dead. As I had grabbed the pen to record the OOD's orders in the log, this sound rumbled through my body, shaking me to my very core. In that moment, however, I wasn't on board a ship. In my mind's eye, the ship was suddenly gone. Instead, I was lying in a baby's crib with wooden slats surrounding me. The feeling that took hold of me in that moment was a sense of absolute terror. This overwhelming fear continued for at least sixty seconds. I stood immobile, practically pulverized, working through my brain and heart the fact that "I'm not in a crib. I'm not an infant. I'm aboard a ship and there is nothing that will harm me."

Within ninety seconds, the fear was gone and never returned. I returned to my duties but was unsettled by the experience and tried to work through what had happened and where those memories came from. Later that day, the root cause of that fear dawned on me. When I was just six weeks old, the U.S. Navy relocated my family from London, England (where I was born), to Newport, Rhode Island. My father was finishing up thirty years in the Navy and Newport was to be his last tour of duty. While living there for the briefest time, we were housed in Newport bay on a tiny island called Goat Island. The naval housing that once stood there has now been replaced by condos and a hotel. But, in 1959, it contained a row of houses and we lived on the far end of that island right next to the foghorn. I remember nothing of that time, but on board that sailing ship eighteen years later I came face-to-face with the long-dormant neural pathways that had formed on Goat Island. The bellowing sound from the foghorn brought it screaming back to me, as it triggered emotions planted in my memory long before words had meaning.

**Conquering the Beliefs That Hold Us Back**

While this one memory came out of the blue, it demonstrates vividly a phenomenon common to the entire human family—and the next emphasis for flipping our focus. All of us have experiences and pick up messages during our lives that we don't intend to acquire. They just come from the act of living. Yet they become unknowingly embedded in our brains and hearts. As in this story, some of these are imposed by our outward environments. But most are osmotically transmitted to us by our parents, siblings, friends, or experiences while we are very young, but also later in life. Like the sound of the foghorn, these messages plant deep within us thoughts and feelings that are called fears, self-defeating behaviors, or dysfunctional paradigms, but for the sake of discussion right now we'll call them limiting beliefs. As an infant, I didn't know that I was developing a limiting belief about foghorns. Deep within my psyche, however, was a belief that their engulfing sound would do me harm. And later in life, once the belief was triggered, I had a choice: to let it continue to influence me or to overcome it. There was no neutral ground.

The clear majority of limiting beliefs, whether acquired in childhood or later in life, are reactions to *perceived* negative experiences or messages. I say perceived because, ironically, the foghorn was not meant to harm me, but to protect my family and me by preventing ships from running aground into our home. But my infant mind didn't understand any of that. All I knew was that sound meant fear, and those fears remained inside of me until they could be brought to the surface of my conscious mind and then overcome. Until then, the memory was buried deep within me as a protective reaction. So it is with all of us; our perception of the message or experience creates the belief within us, and that belief then dictates our actions around that subject ... unless we become aware of and actively challenge it.

Later in life I was confronted with a limiting belief that had the potential to be equally as paralyzing—but much more dangerous: the belief that I could not work for myself. On a cool February afternoon, some ten years ago, the general counsel for the surgical center and acute care hospital I was CEO of came into my office and informed me that I was no longer employed there. Just a year earlier, I had helped these two entities navigate away from the brink of bankruptcy back to profitability. Now, that was over.

With the same fear I had experienced upon hearing the foghorn, the process of "finding" my next job began. All my life I had worked for someone else, and I told myself this time was going to be no different. As I set about submitting résumés and interviewing for new positions (because if your limiting belief is "I work for someone else," that's what you do—look somewhere else), I had a visit with my oldest son, Adam, who was twenty-three at the time and in many ways wiser than his age. It's awesome when that happens with your kids. Adam looked at me and asked, "Dad, have you ever considered working for yourself?" The thought petrified me. I told myself I liked the security of having a paycheck and building on ground someone else had put there. Fear flushed over my face as I replied, "I could never do that." To which he replied, "You may not know it, but you are an entrepreneur. You are an independent thinker."

My job search was going slow, and about a month later Adam and I had another conversation. He asked me if I had thought more about our last talk. I told him I had, but working for myself "just wasn't me." In a moment, like what transpired between Yoda and Luke Skywalker in *Star Wars*, I heard my son say, "The trouble is, you've got to learn to let go of the limiting beliefs you have about yourself. Find the intersection of your knowledge, your experience, and your passion *and play there.* This is your sweet spot, and when you figure that out, work is fun … *and money finds you."*

While these thoughts were spinning through my head, I began being contacted by doctors I knew and being asked for some "help" with their practices. I enjoyed being engaged in something productive, and found that providing this help was fun. Months later, still looking for a job but finding myself busier and busier with this "help"—which had a new name: "consulting"—I still couldn't accept the idea of working for myself because it conflicted with the "identity" I had in my head. Unlike the two minutes it took to overcome the fear of the foghorn, this limiting belief was holding on with a mighty force.

The final piece of the puzzle fell into place when one day I came across a book by Richard Barrett, a former World Bank executive, entitled *A Guide to Liberating Your Soul.* What struck me in his book was this simple but profound thought: all of us are here on this earth with a unique gift that our soul desires to fulfill. Barrett called it "our soul's purpose." We find that gift by searching out those experiences that give us an inner sense of fulfillment while doing something for someone else. Our ego, on the other hand, doesn't care about any mission. It is seeking power, position, wealth, and security. And, like a petulant child, ego hangs on for dear life. We only embrace the purpose of our soul, however, by letting go of ego. Once you achieve this, something remarkable takes place. As if it had been waiting for this moment to happen, Providence clears the way with a stream of events and assistance you never dreamed would come your way. In fact, you no longer have a career -- your work becomes your mission.

As I absorbed this message, the moment came to finally let go of that limiting belief, and like the sound of the foghorn, the fear within that limiting belief has never returned.

**Limiting Beliefs Create Our Boundaries to What Is Possible**

From my experience, all emotionally adjusted adults build numerous shields around their hearts to protect themselves from fear, pain, embarrassment, experiences, or messages we had in the past that we choose not to repeat. These shields become the boundaries of our limiting beliefs. But, like a scientist who discovers a new breakthrough, we experience one of the greatest moments in life once we realize we will never go past the boundaries of our own personal limiting beliefs—unless we actively challenge and dismantle them. Indeed, left untouched, they create the fences and borders of our comfort zone, they establish the boundaries of our reality, and we view anything beyond them as outside our reach or, like the foghorn, even dangerous. Truly, our body will not go where our mind and heart have not already been. Until I eliminated the belief I could not work for myself, I never would. But once that belief was gone … oh the world of possibilities that opened!

All wise leaders eventually reach a point in life where they stop blaming others, as discussed in the last chapter, look at themselves honestly and see the results of what they have created. At that point, they ask searching questions like, "What is tripping me up? How do I conquer these almost demon-like factors that continue to hold me back?" This is a time of conscious incompetence—a realization that there are internal factors acting as limits, and yet they appear beyond our ability to recognize or change.

**Countering the Negative Voices**

Ending the blame game is the start of countering these negative voices. None of the rest matters if we are not willing to take personal responsibility for where we are, both the good and the bad. This sets the stage to begin to recognize those things that have been holding us back, and are still holding us back today. Like hearing the foghorn, this is a point where there is no more neutral ground. We either continue to allow the limiting beliefs to keep us where we are, or we hold them up one at a time to the light of day and set about getting rid of them.

Our limiting beliefs come in many forms. For example, they may contain messages concerning relationships, money, negotiations, dealing with contention, providing feedback, raising children, our ability to change, and whether or not we accept that we have the freedom to choose. Self-imposed limits may also be found in our perceptions of the economy, money, people, wealth, status, success, schooling, love, family, or whether or not we see opportunity in problems. Whatever they are and wherever they reside within us, leaders must acquire the skill to recognize and challenge them—or else they will stunt our personal and organizational growth.

## Identifying Limiting Beliefs

While the two examples of my own limiting beliefs were brought to the forefront of my mind and heart by outside events, we can also take steps to consciously identify the limiting beliefs we hold onto. I've found most limiting beliefs are wrapped up in self-talk phrases that contain the words "can't," "won't," "shouldn't," "if only," or "when I." And, tying back to chapter 3, through careful introspection we can also spot them anytime we fall into the mode of accusing, blaming, or criticizing. Every one contains a negative message that de-energizes us and limits our potential.

Once we do recognize one of our limiting beliefs, examining the root message or experience that put it there in the first place allows us to challenge the truth of that moment and then actively overcome it. The foghorn was just such a moment for me, clearing away the fog in my heart that had settled there for over eighteen years.

## Identifying Limiting Beliefs, Take 2

Here's another way to discover some of your most pressing limiting beliefs. Put the book down and list as many frustrations as you can in ninety seconds. Be sure to write full statements, not just a word like "spouse" or "employees." For example, a single mom in one of my seminars wrote: "There is not enough time in the day," "My divorce is taking too long," and "My dog won't stop running away."

Then, with your list of frustrations in hand, circle the top two and ask yourself these questions about each:

1. What boundary does this place on me?
2. Where do I think this frustration came from?
3. What if this situation weren't true? What possibilities might that open up?
4. What can I do to take personal responsibility to overcome this belief and get past it?

### The Voice of Failure

Dealing with the subconscious memories from foghorns is one thing, but uncovering and then dismantling the boundaries and walls we have erected and are influenced by each day is another. How do we go about challenging and eradicating the more pervasive and damaging limiting beliefs that hold us back every day? One particularly common and destructive limiting belief I would like to focus on concerns failure and the perception that it is a sign of incompetence—something that indicates a person is incapable and not worthwhile. In our Western culture, this perception is reinforced by school systems, parents, siblings, peers, and the workforce.

Yet this is a false paradigm. Further, it's among the most damaging limiting beliefs that must be overcome if we are to become strong leaders and our best selves. Simply by looking at history we can see that success is found in the seeds of failure. 99.99% of self-made men and women can point to a profound failure in their life that became a turning point and springboard for their future success. They discover it is the lessons and not the losses that count, and while we cannot go back in time and create a new start, we can create new beginnings.

Thomas Edison, for example, is lauded today as one of the greatest inventors of all time. He was awarded a record 1,093 patents in his lifetime. His work included the creation of the phonograph, motion picture cameras, and the incandescent lightbulb—along with the creation of an electrical delivery system that would make the use of the lightbulb safe and economical. The story is told that while experimenting to find the right filament that would transmit light, Edison was asked by a reporter how it felt knowing he had tried over 1,000 different filaments ... yet none worked so far. Edison simply replied, "Well, at least I know a thousand ways that don't work." Not everything Edison developed was a success. The talking doll, electronic vote recorder, electric pen, and use of cement to build everything from pianos to cabinets were commercial failures. Yet these are minor footnotes in his life because he never let failure get in the way of his next success. Rather, he saw each failure as a springboard to his next achievement.

### *Failure Is a Key to Success—If We Allow It*

During the gut-wrenching, soul-searching time after I was let go as a CEO, my son Adam did one more thing for me. He shared a very impactful book: *Outwitting the Devil*, by Napoleon Hill. Hill was one of the very first authors to dive into the minds of the very successful at the turn of the twentieth century. His classic *Think and Grow Rich* was first published in 1937 and is still in publication today. It is considered "the granddaddy of all motivational literature." His final book to be published, *Outwitting the Devil*, was published forty years after his death as he had requested. It is a fitting bookend for his life, the summary of his life's research and work. After interviewing an array of successful people, he realized something important: *Every one of them had experienced profound failure at one point in their life—and had learned to overcome it.* With no exception, they viewed their failure as key to their success because the fear of failure no longer had control over them. In the preamble to the book, Hill wrote,

> *Fear is the tool of a man-made devil. Self-confident faith in one's self is both the man-made weapon which defeats the devil and the man-made tool which builds a triumphant life. And it is more than that. It is a link to the irresistible forces of the universe which stand behind a man who does not believe in failure and defeat as being anything but temporary experiences.*

For me, Hills words have proved prophetic and true on all counts. Before launching a consulting firm, God took me to the door of consulting two other times. Both times I declined because I felt my kids were too young for their dad to be on the road. But the third time, He kicked me through the door with cowboy boots on and there was no turning back. For almost a year, we lived on beans, rice, and (providentially) an introductory mortgage rate. And the "irresistible forces" Hill alludes to worked in my life ever so slowly, and effectively. Genuine failure became the springboard for success and happiness, fulfillment and reward. I work harder now than I ever have, but most days it does not feel like work. True to the words of Richard Barrett, the work I am engaged in feels like a mission, not a job. It is almost all joy.

One of the most profound ways we can flip our focus as leaders is to release ourselves, and our teams, from this fear of failure. When the fear of failure permeates a business, the results are automatically limiting—no risks are taken, and no growth is experienced. Employees are protective and do only what they are told to do, management is suspicious, and mistrust is deeply felt. It is a vicious, downward cycle. Much like the Hillcrest Knights under Coach Smith who had the habit of grinding mistakes into the players' faces, this fear destabilizes an organization and everyone is just "looking out for themselves," as one Hillcrest player described that era. But when a leader and an organization adopts a new focus, and accepts that mistakes will be made—and learned from—paradoxically the path to advancement and improvement is certain. Once, when the founder of Honda Motor Company was asked about the key to his success, he replied, "I made as many mistakes as fast as I could." And his positive attitude permeated the culture—and laid the foundation for the company Honda is today. Why? Because mistakes lead to the ques- tions, and the *right* questions lead to progress.

**Perfection or Excellence?**

In today's society that seeks perfection and does not accept failure, how do we view failure in this positive way when our limiting beliefs are screaming out in disappointment and disbelief? My limiting beliefs certainly were yelling as the bills stacked up and cash flow was tight when launching my business. I am indebted to my dear wife Judene for her patience and belief in me, and to the encouragement of my son Adam and the lessons and resources he shared with me along the way. I am also indebted to my dear friend and colleague Travis Anderson, owner of Strategic Leadership Consulting, for a new paradigm about failure that truly helped win this battle in my own life. He explained to me over twenty-five years ago that our perception of failure is tied directly to whether we are focused on achieving perfection *or* excellence.

As Travis explained, perfectionism is a myth because it cannot be obtained. Yet many of us believe that if we *look* perfect, it will somehow shield us from pain and bring us happiness. However, it does not actually provide a pathway to success, happiness, or a life free of pain because perfectionism limits our potential rather than expands it. In an insightful conversation, Travis shared how perfectionism doesn't accept risk, is concerned with how you look, is based on fear, and will not permit mistakes. The quest for perfection is solely focused on control and external power. With it, there is never enough of anything—and it is focused on playing not to lose. As Travis laid this out before me, I realized I grew up with this limiting belief called perfectionism. And like the habit of blaming, it is a dead-end street.

There is another path, however, and it is full of possibilities because it puts you on a trajectory of growth and progress. As Travis taught me, this path is called excellence. It accepts risk and knows that we grow THE MOST from our mistakes . Excellence is concerned with doing good, is centered on hope, and is focused on influence, internal power, and finding gratitude even when life is hard and things look bleak. What's more, when excellence is our goal, we are looking forward, accepting the lessons from the past but not the lim- its.

### *It's the Lessons, and Not the Losses, That Count*

In my experience, true joy in life comes when we go to the edge of our limiting beliefs, embrace the truth that it is the lessons and not the losses that count, and then with clarity and fortitude charge ahead. When we do, the forces of the universe begin to leverage our efforts and create a way forward that is both challenging and miraculous. Indeed, once we possess clarity of vision, know what we want, are fully committed to that outcome, and refuse to listen to the naysayers, it is as if the universe suddenly shifts and various forces now cooperate and harmonize on our behalf.

Such progress will not transpire when we hold on to the idea that everything we do must be perfect, but it can take place with the forward-looking and hope-filled mindset of excellence. This is a way of thinking and seeing the world that empowers leaders to set the stage for teams to be their best and to create organizations and lives of significance. The top-down model of leadership uses control to enforce a false paradigm of perfection. The upside-down approach, however, isn't looking for perfection and doesn't need authoritarian control. Instead, with excellence as the goal, the upside-down leader becomes the catalyst for personal and organizational growth, ever-expanding influence, and unbounded success.

**Coach's Challenge**

1. Looking back on your life, how have failures helped define you more than successes?
2. What important lessons have you internalized through failure that you would have missed with success?
3. Looking forward, how will you allow your failures to lead you to success?
4. What are a few of the most vocal limiting beliefs inside you? How can you challenge them to overcome them?
5. How can you keep a positive mindset when failures in your life occur?
6. Will you let go of perfectionism and do your best to understand and accept yourself as a being capable of excellence?

CHAPTER SIX:

# Delegate (Almost) Everything — But Vision, Direction, and Pace

*Lesson: Leaders let their team become their hands.*

**What Got You Here Won't Keep You Here**

For the majority of business leaders, the idea they should delegate control and power, even in small amounts to their team, is a foreign thought. Most small business owners are successful in their early years because they are terrific "doers" and have a great work ethic and customer service drive. They believe their success has come because of control, not empowerment, and in the early stages of a small business that may be what is needed.

But a company quickly outgrows this style of hands-on leadership, and if it persists as the organization grows, the company will stall in its progress, plateau, and then begin to falter because what got you to where you are today is not what is going to get you where you need to be tomorrow.

**Case Study: The Paradox of Letting Go to Move Forward**

After two years of coaching, a client was still repeatedly struggling with this concept. This man was a brilliant technician, and his ability and quality-minded work led to the creation of a successful business. Doing things well with his hands built a million-dollar business from scratch, and he personally received great joy from completing tasks and accomplishing technical work. The problem was this success came with a cost. As the business grew and customers multiplied, the demands grew as well, and years of sixteen-hour days eventually led to health troubles and burnout. Even so, he seemed frozen in his ability to bring other professionals on and delegate effectively to them.

We spent many coaching sessions discussing the conceptual and practical side of this key leadership element, but the conversations were ultimately unproductive. Finally, during one onsite coaching session, I asked him to close his eyes for about three minutes. This is the scenario painted for him to imagine:

> *It is a Friday afternoon and you are driving back to the office after visiting your clinic thirty minutes away. While stopped at an intersection for a red light, you notice the car coming behind you is approaching way too fast. There is no way you are going to avoid an accident if you don't think quickly. You see an opening in the traffic in front of you, but misjudge the speed of the car racing behind you. As you dart into the intersection, the car behind you rams into your rear end, hurtling your car into cars in front of you. You hold onto the steering wheel to keep from losing control; airbags deploy as the car finally comes to a stop. You are alive but your car is totaled. Worse yet, there is a profound pain shooting from both arms as you realize that your left and right arms have compound fractures. They will take months to heal.*
>
> *You now have two days to determine how your business is going to not only survive but thrive without the use of your hands. What will you do different now?*

As my client opened his eyes, there was a change in his demeanor. He wasn't fighting this anymore. He had gone through the scenario in his mind and was <u>emotionally</u> ready to save his business. We began discussing all the changes that would need to take place by Monday morning if this scenario were true. Ideas continued to flow and we outlined a path for success. We spent at least two hours on this activity, continually asking questions and formulating plans. During the exercise, I even asked him to sit on his hands so he fully recognized they were not free to be used.

In those two hours, a lightbulb turned on in his mind and heart. Suddenly, he could see the path of empowerment. And since that discussion, he has become a brand-new leader. He broke through the limiting beliefs that he could not and did not want to delegate, to a new realization that he receives true joy from seeing the "hands" of his team go to work. And these changes have also transformed his schedule—he has gone from never being home to being home weeknights and weekends, while benefiting his health and his business (which grew by more than 30 percent in one year after this breakthrough.) His story serves as a great example of what can come from igniting people, performance, and profits.

**The Lazy—and Ineffective—Leadership Mindset**

As my client experienced before this breakthrough, burnout is quite real and common among business owners. Desks and calendars become full of tasks, many of which could be delegated to team members. Too often, however, saddled with the limiting belief that "No one can do it better than me" or "It's faster if I just do it rather than show someone else how," a business owner becomes, as was mentioned in the beginning of the book, a "chief everything officer" and in the process becomes overworked, ineffective, and tapped out.

A leader might hold tight to these limiting beliefs because to do so demands nothing new. They allow us to remain in our comfort zone of just doing more of the same. But the result is like what happens when parents decide to clean up after their toddler because it's "easier" that way. In the end their child isn't growing, and the parents become increasingly frustrated when they don't establish the boundaries that teach their child responsibility. Likewise—as hard as this point is—often, it is laziness that causes a leader and owner to adopt a mindset that "No one can do it better than me" or the corollary "I'm the only one who can do it because I'm the owner of the business." Occasionally, I also encounter owners who refuse to let go because of the ego-stroking that takes place as they continue to single-handedly keep the business growing. It can be very validating to be the person everyone and everything must flow "through," but it is also a precursor to personal and organizational struggles.

**Look at Your Desk**

Even when owners tell me they are good at delegating, I suggest evaluating this through one simple benchmark exercise: making a detailed list of what is on their desk. Try it yourself right now for ten minutes. Just grab a piece of paper and make a list of (1) the items that are there, (2) the demands they represent, and (3) the projects you're working on.

Now, with that list in hand, go through it item by item asking this question: Am I *really* the only one who can do this? Be completely open and honest with your answers. Afterward, step back and see what remains on your list. Most leaders find, more often than not, 80–90 percent of the things on their desk could be delegated to other members of their team if they effectively invested the time and the training in team members to be trustworthy with the assignment. And talk about return on investment—this delegation would then allow the leaders to perform their very highest and best work: growing the boundaries of their organization, facilitating change, and leading their team ensuring they are all engaged in doing their highest and best as well. (The keys to effective delegation will be explored in detail in chapter 7. For now, just know that effective delegation is more than simply giving an employee a list of things to do. It also isn't putting someone in a position and hoping they will "catch on" through on-the-job training.)

**So ... What Can't Be Delegated?**

As Jim Faber shared with me years ago, the ultimate task of an upside-down leader is to create a team of trustworthy, well-trained, well-equipped, and superbly empowered team members—and then to get out of their way. This means ultimately delegating (almost) everything. I say "almost" because there are certain things that by their very nature cannot be delegated. Based upon the business, there may be areas of expertise the business owner performs that are his or hers alone to do. But even in these situations, as with my client in the earlier story, most of these areas of expertise could also be delegated to the right person or group of people.

But, experience shows me the following three things cannot be delegated and are instinctively the job of a leader:

- establishing the vision
- marking the direction
- and setting the pace of your organization

Why is this the leader's responsibility? As discussed earlier, humans are hierarchical beings and respond to social structure. We know intuitively that the leader of an organization is the one who sets the vision, direction, and pace. This cannot be effectively delegated to anyone else. Others may aid with this, but in the end, like the sign on President Truman's desk, "The Buck Stops Here" when it comes to these three leadership fundamentals.

**Creating a Vision for You and Your Team**

The good news is it's not difficult to establish a vision and direction. It does, however, require clarity of mind, thought, and emotion—and it takes time.

Vision and direction is a picture of tomorrow. Like a nation's constitution, through words and emotion, it establishes where a group is going, how they are going to get there—and why it even matters. All three elements are critical because they establish the cultural foundation of a group and let others know what success looks like. For your vision statement to be powerful, it must come from the heart and it must be relevant to you and your goals for the future. Again, no one else can or should be asked to do this for you. That may seem contrary to the entire idea of being an upside-down leader, yet experience has shown it is one thing you must define for yourself and the group. Doing so creates clarity. Without it, there's anarchy.

And one warning about creating a meaningful vision for your organization: If your vision is primarily defined by dollar signs, the vision will be unsustainable. The acquisition of money is a by-product that comes with successfully implementing a deeply held, inspiring personal vision. Money itself is not a motivator that brings about exceptional performance, though it can be a reward for exceptional personal performance.

### Writing Your Vision Statement

If you haven't taken the time to pen your vision statement, what is holding you back? As my good friend Art McCracken and I co-authored in an article a few years ago in the Progressive Dentist, the process starts by asking these clarifying questions:

1. What is my cause and what am I passionate about? (i.e., What really gets me up in the morning, and what am I deep-down excited about?)
2. What is the present and future path of my business—and is it clearly defined in my mind and heart?
3. Does my team understand their roles in this vision? Do they share that same passion?

Now, with these ideas in place, begin to write about what you want in your personal and professional life—and in the lives of your team members:

1. Knowing what you know now: if you could start over today, what would you change? What would that specifically look

like? What would it specifically feel like?
2. In all honesty, who would you bring with you? Who would you leave behind?
3. What type of services do you feel a true connection and passion for providing? What would you provide to patients?
4. What experiences would you be willing to fight for on behalf of your customers and/or your team?
5. Now, having identified the team members you would bring along, what role would they play in this vision? What would it look and feel like to them?
6. In what ways can you be more involved at all levels in your organization and the community it serves?

Fundamentally, a well-written vision statement will define three things well:

- Who are you?
- What do you do?
- How do you do it and why?

The answers don't have to be lengthy. But they do need to be inspirational and clarifying. To gauge this, after having answered these questions, review what you have and then ask yourself:

1. Does it create a level of excitement inside of me?
2. Does it ring true to my core belief system and desires for the future?
3. Does it provide me and my team a reason to exist and work hard together?

If you can answer "yes" to these questions, you have a vision statement with power.

**Case Study: Learning to Get Out of the Way**

To provide a closing example of the principles in this chapter, let me introduce you to Dr. Mike Hamilton. He purchased his practice from two doctors, combined two teams, and brought them together as a brand-new graduate from dental school. At first it seemed that he was trying to do it all alone. His desk was piled high and his hours were very, very long. When I met him, he wanted to know how to stop being a chief everything officer and instead become his company's chief empowerment officer, ensuring that everyone on his team was working at their very highest ability and doing their best, that they were delegated to appropriately, and that they honored what was delegated.

We started at the beginning, he and I working on vision and direction: the whys and the hows, and what they were going to provide for their patients that was unique.

Then, once Dr. Hamilton's vision and direction were clearly laid out, he went through the process of clarifying his own expectations, establishing the roles and goals of every team member—while understanding the metrics that define the success behind each goal, which will be discussed more in chapter 7.

With this homework complete, he shared these with the entire team and he did an exceptional job. The results of his planning and visionary work were phenomenal: A team that had never worked together quickly became a solid unit with an attitude of enthusiasm, purpose, and passion. A year later they are an exceptional group of professionals. Dr. Hamilton continues to wrestle with things on his desk, but he reduced his hours, increased the practice's productivity by over 30–40 percent compared to the previous owners, and gave up most of the babysitting that was hampering him at first. His team is successful because, first and foremost, he accepted his role as a leader to set the vision and direction – and then followed through with its implementation come what may.

### *Leaders Also Set the Pace*

In addition to vision and direction, there is one other thing that leaders cannot delegate, and that is pace—the internal rhythm and tempo of an organization. Pace is a direct reflection of a leader's own internal sense of urgency to accomplish his or her vision. It is felt as well as communicated, and seems to be both directly as well as osmotically conveyed.

As explained in chapter 1, organizations cannot run faster than their leader. Therefore, when a leader hastens the pace, the organization does as well. Conversely, if a leader becomes ineffective through stress, burnout, lack of vision, or mistrust, the pace of an organization can slow to a halt.

Think of leaders setting the pace much like a conductor of an orchestra sets the tempo for a symphony. How fast or slow the orchestra plays is up to the person up front. But it takes intuition and judgment to set a pace that is appropriate for the present need. If the pace is too fast, then teams get burned out. If the pace is too slow, forward movement and momentum dies. This is where clarity in the mind of the leader, and up-front communication with team members is vital.

Beware that leaders can also outpace their teams if they assume everyone should be able to work at their breakneck speed. Balance is needed, and a vision of the timeline—whether this is a 100-yard dash, a 26-mile marathon, or a 5K intermediate run—must be understood by all.

For Dr. Hamilton to grow as dramatically as he did in his first year of ownership, the pace he set was a definite change from that of his predecessors. His clearly articulated vision and direction dictated the pace, and it was his own personal sense of urgency that made the pace a reality. He was careful, however, to ensure he didn't outpace his team. Through well-planned team and individual coaching, effective communication, training, and system development, he kept his team right in step with himself, and everyone shared in the pride (and reward) of accomplishing something that hadn't been done before.

**Finding the Highest and Best for All**

What does it take for your team to take on the work and projects you are involved in right now? It begins with the upside-down leader mindset. Then through hiring, training, motivating, and communication skills, the tasks become owned by capable team members. This then permits you to focus on your very highest and best activities—the ones that only you can do but often find there is no time for because of all the other things you are absorbed in.

In the book, Good to Great, Jim Collins describes the importance of getting the right people and the right team on the right seats on "the bus." Finding the right seats for your team members boils down to this: what is their highest and best? What position of responsibility and authority can they be given to both use their very best capabilities within and then to allow those capabilities to complement the skills and strengths of everybody else? We do a disservice to others when we do not give them an opportunity to do their best. Leadership is about determining how you capture that best in order to leverage the time and capability of everybody on the team.

Does the process of setting this in motion require a very real investment of time, energy, and money? Certainly. Chapters 7, 8, and 9 dive deeply into this, describing the steps of setting clear expectations and accountability, creating a culture of genuine participation and ownership, and fueling this culture with appropriate appreciation. But the tremendous payback of time, energy, and money makes the investment worthwhile. And surpassing your vision, while being surrounded by a team of self-directed champions, is the greatest reward of all.

**Coach's Challenge**

1. What must change in your business that will allow you to train your employees and delegate tasks so you can focus on your primary goals as a leader?
2. If you haven't done so before, spend an hour thinking out loud with two or three trusted advisors answering these questions: "What do we do? How do we do it? And why are we doing it?" Don't accept superficial replies, but dig deep and find succinct and powerful answers.
3. If you have trouble fulfilling your true role as a leader, what must change so you can seek the help needed to accomplish it?
4. Will you get out of the way of your employees and help them grow to fulfill their full potential? How will you do this?
5. Will you examine the projects or tasks on your desk to see which assignments can be delegated to others? What must be done now to delegate these? Create a list detailing these action items, the person you will delegate the project or task to, and by when. Then, arrive at a follow up mechanism for each and how it will be used for both you and your team member for clarity and ownership.

# IT'S FED BY COACHING & TEACHING

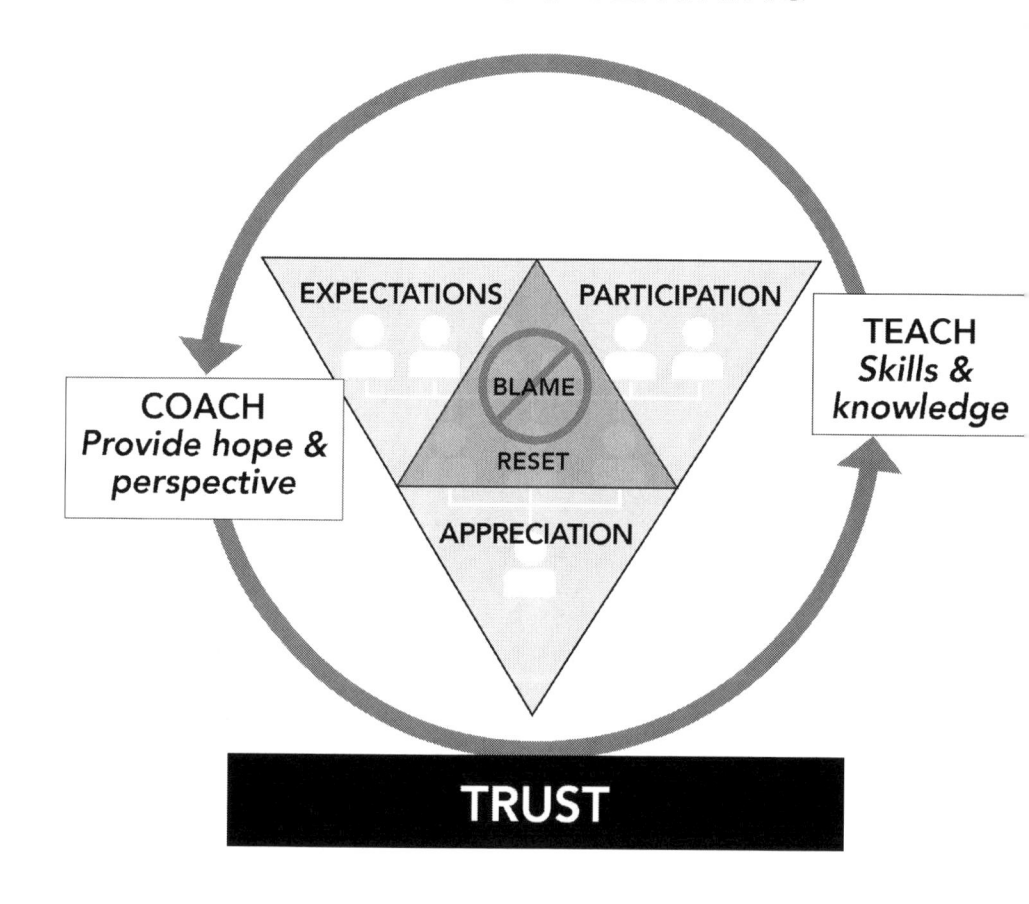

**COACH**
*Provide hope & perspective*

**EXPECTATIONS**

**PARTICIPATION**

**BLAME** 🚫
**RESET**

**APPRECIATION**

**TEACH**
*Skills & knowledge*

**TRUST**

CHAPTER SEVEN:

# A Total Commitment to Your Team's Success

*Lesson: Leaders create other leaders.*

One of the foundational truths taught in *The Seven Habits of Highly Effective People* is that to make profound change in your life, you must shift your paradigms. Yes, we can nibble around the edges of our life by working on our attitudes. But there is only one way to create quantum change, and that is through having a complete "shift" of our views and thoughts pertaining to a subject—to literally flip our focus. The entire way we approach life, and its challenges and opportunities, is based upon our paradigms.

Each chapter in this book presents a fundamental shift in how we view leadership and the role leaders take. And each shift moves us closer toward not only thinking about leadership in an entirely new way but also *leading* in a new way, because when someone moves on the inside, they can't help but move on the outside.

So far we have focused on growth inside of you. This chapter now lays out what the start of that *outside* growth and movement looks like for you. We do this by discussing the first day-to-day, hands-on components of upside-down leadership. It starts with the mindset to work yourself out of your present job.

**Working Yourself Out of a Job**

The phrase "work yourself out of a job" is another leadership paradox. At face value, it seems opposite to all the gut instincts of a business owner. But just like in basketball, where great rebounders learn to move away from the ball instead of toward it, only by doing so can you ensure your ultimate success as an organization. And how is it done? Once again, by flipping your focus. The words of John Wooden, the famed UCLA basketball coach from the 1960s who guided his team to a record ten NCAA national championships, says it all: "Think of yourself as a *teacher*." That shift in frame of reference from being a boss to a teacher, from being an enforcer to a motivator, from requiring to inspiring, is the mindset that helps make upside-down leadership happen.

The first kind of teaching is skill-based, and far too often in small businesses this is not given the attention it deserves. Whether the position is one that can be filled by the newest entry to the job market or requires someone with seniority and experience, skill-based teaching should follow this mantra: how do we "tee" this team member up for success? A clearly defined learning "plan" is the place to start with specific objectives, key outcomes, and time for the lessons to settle in before duties are expanded further. Using the phrase "Begin with the end in mind" is very helpful in creating such a plan: defining what success looks like and then working backward to to-day—each time asking the question "How do we train to create this outcome?" and making sure the plan is in writing and shared with all involved.

The second type of teaching is even more powerful than skill-based training because it gets to the root of the culture of the organization. I wrote earlier of the type of organization Jim Faber established when I worked for him over thirty years ago. *The Seven Habits of Highly Effective People* became our curriculum, teaching each other became part of the culture, and discussing the lessons we were picking up, and what they meant to us, became part of our daily walk and talk. Each week we had management meetings and management training. We discussed business needs but also made sure we invested time in self-education. Jim spent a good amount of time teaching, but he also ensured his team members had specific responsibilities and time for teaching each other as well. And through this process, the concepts discussed started to lodge in our hearts, create quantum changes in our minds, and affected the way we worked together, managed time, defined success, and led our teams.

This same model of regular, consistent group teaching became the template for teaching at Franklin Quest and PageNet, as well. After taming the operational crises at both locations, Jim's example was followed with facilitated Friday afternoon management team trainings on the Seven Habits. These included teaching and discussing one chapter (or often a part of a chapter) each week as well as some creative experiential games to help drive home the many points. The constant focus on this as a leadership team helped put us all on the same page intellectually and culturally, while reinforcing the value placed on these concepts.

Whether you use the Seven Habits as a curriculum, or other means of training, the key is to have a clear agenda and objectives when meeting with your leadership team. It's also critical to realize that effecting real change takes time. This is not a flash-in-the-pan continuing education course that motivates and then is filed away on a shelf. This training must be a consistent drumbeat that builds on itself and involves the entire management team. Most team members will find upside-down leadership and organizations a refreshing new change, but a change all the same and will need time to adjust. Because of prevailing workplace cultures, some may even view a leader as a teacher with suspicion. But the good news is that feelings of empowerment go far to inspire and excite the people who work for you—and with consistency, teaching, and congruent behavior, teams climb on board quickly.

### The Transfacilitative Leader™

The term I use to describe this level of leader interaction with one's team is "transfacilitative leadership." Transformation of your team is the goal. Your role is to help facilitate this change by defining clear growth and cultural outcomes, establishing a plan, getting everyone involved, and leading the charge. Taking this on may seem intimidating at first, but there are few leadership activities more important than lifting one's team to a higher level through personally teaching and training them. The side impact to leaders, in addition to raising the bar for their team, is it raises the bar for themselves. You cannot teach something and then feel good about ignoring it. And the teacher always gets more out of material than the students.

This culture of teaching did not stop at the management level. In addition to the weekly training, time was set aside every month for training the entire organization using the same outcome-focused approach. Every six months or so we also had special trainings led by guest lecturers, or dedicated fun events, such as an employee outdoor "Olympics" we held annually. All of this just became a part of "how we do things," knowing that staying sharp means continually sharpening the saw. Just like a sharp blade cuts everything better, a sharp mind approaches everything with more creativity. Training is an absolute must when you are committed to your team's success. It is a fundamental way you work yourself out of a job.

### *One-on-Ones*

In addition to group training, other training opportunities come in the form of frequent one-on-one coaching sessions with each member on a leader's team. As we've discussed, leading upside-down means fundamentally doing things differently. One-on-ones are another significant difference from what often occurs in organizations operating from the traditional top-down perspective. Where in those organizations this level of one-on-one communication is often limited to annual performance reviews—which, at best, end up being neutral and are almost always dreaded by everyone involved—the one-on-ones recommended in upside-down leading are a critical opportunity to put the two types of CARE we discussed in Chapter 3 into concrete action.

The format for a one-on-ones is simple: it is a time for a team member to set pertinent individual goals, review progress toward goals already set, and receive coaching and feedback from his or her leader. It is also a time for the leader to ask for coaching and feedback in return. At the end of the session, the leader wraps up the discussion by encouraging, instilling confidence in the team member, and expressing appreciation. Keeping a written record of what was discussed is important for follow-ups during subsequent one-on-ones. Scheduling these meetings ahead of time is an absolute, and ensuring they are kept is vital. I found that out the hard way when some of my team members communicated that my being late to, or not keeping these coaching sessions, told them I didn't value them as much as my words said.

The objectives behind one on ones are many. The first is to further develop the trust between the leader and the team member by interacting at a personal level. When a leader shows genuine interest in the development and progress of a team member, that is powerful stuff. When all elements of CARE are used by the leader, then great things happen in that relationship. One-on-ones are a genuine opportunity to employ all eight parts of CARE. And when these are used consistently and with intent, it fosters and deepens trust. Barriers drop. Rapport is gained. Loyalty is won. Another purpose is to ensure that individual team members clearly understand the expectations of their role and know how they are performing so performance reviews do not generate surprises.

*Teaching Is Not Helicoptering*

The opportunities to teach and train as a leader are almost endless. What is described here are some formal approaches to this through skill-based training, weekly management training, monthly team training, and one-on-ones. Naturally, teaching also takes place every day through frequent interactions. We must be careful, however, to ensure the teaching does not become helicopter management through hovering, micromanaging, and not allowing mistakes. As discussed in chapter 3, mistakes are part of the process of improvement if they are captured, discussed, learned from, and then corrected.

When we talk about leaders "getting out of the way," it means getting out of the way of yourself and getting out of the way of your team. You do this by being a catalyst, promoting growth within each member of your team through establishing clear goals, and seeing they receive the training needed to succeed. This also requires consistent follow-up with team members, offering personal mentoring to reinforce their goals and training.

## Getting the Needed Tools

Another highly significant way leaders work themselves out of a job, while expanding their organization, is to seek the resources (AKA tools) needed for their teams to succeed.

With the variety of tools available in any industry (and sales people who are skilled at promoting their tool), it can be a challenge to know where to invest hard-earned dollars for tools that will achieve the goals above while also providing a return on investment. This is where doing your homework up front makes a difference.

*To Buy or Not to Buy? How to Think Through and Research Your Options*

The purpose of doing homework or research when you're considering buying a new tool for your business is to create clarity:

What specifically is the defined outcome for acquiring this tool, and what are the criteria for making the decision?

Here's a method to help with this process:
1. Begin by defining the outcome in writing. This critical step creates the mental benchmark for success.
2. Next, brainstorm the criteria that are factors in the decision. Here are some examples:
    a. Does it make work faster?
    b. Does it make work easier?
    c. Would it help us be more efficient?
    d. Is it of higher quality than our current tool?
    e. Does it make work more fun?
3. Once the criteria are thoroughly listed, separate the criteria into two categories: givens and wants.

Givens are absolutes. Either the option at hand meets them or it doesn't. If it doesn't, it's a strikeout.

Wants, however, are ranked on a scale of 1–10 because not every want is equal. Then, each option under consideration is scored based on how well it meets each want on a scale of 1–10.

4. A final, simple process of multiplying the importance of each want by how well each individual option meets it provides the final benchmark in determining if this option is worthwhile— or which option is best when comparing many different options.

**Investing in the Right Tools**

While at Franklin Quest, I had the chance to serve on a small executive team was charged with making the final decision of a significant purchase: a multi-million-dollar technological system that would improve the accuracy and speed of all customer shipments. We also had to ensure that the system could handle ever-increasing capacity needs. How did we make this important decision? Two senior level executives, an IT colleague, and I had just toured the Spokane, Washington, facility offering an option we were considering. Now back at our hotel, we took Post-it Notes and markers and got to work clarifying the issues and factors involved. First, we wrote down the goals for this acquisition. Then, we listed the decision criteria and sorted them by what were the givens and what were the things we wanted out of this purchase. Once this was done and we had completed our discussion, the right choice was evident. The decision fell out quickly, roughly an hour after completing our tour. A matter that had been weighing on the four of us for months was met with clarity—and the result of this clarity was even more gratifying. Once the project was completed a year later, we surpassed our goals.

**Leaders Create Other Leaders**

I'd like to close this chapter by identifying the second test or defining characteristic of a leader, a feature that helps foster growth in your team. We discussed the first— Leaders don't blame; leaders solve—back in chapter 3. The second characteristic is this: Leaders create other leaders. That's what some of my mentors did, particularly Dennis Webb, Neil Merrill, and Jim Faber. They could look at their team members and see the seeds of greatness. And they took it upon themselves to water and nourish those seeds to sprout and grow, to seek the sunlight, and they continued to encourage them until they finally took root and became leaders in their own right. These mentors sought to work themselves out of a job by leading upside down. By doing this, they accomplished something much more enduring than creating a successful business: in the process, they changed lives forever.

**Coach's Challenge**

1. What needs to change inside to view yourself more as a teacher instead of a boss?
2. Gauge the effectiveness of your present team meetings. How can they become mission critical events? How will you go about making time for training meetings and fun events to keep your employees' minds sharp, focused, and enthusiastic?
3. Bring out your calendar and set the date for your very first one-on-ones. And then schedule the follow-ups as well. Commit to being punctual to these appointments to show your team members that you value and appreciate them.
4. What difference would it make in your business and your life by getting out of the way of your team? Find ways you can do this through (1) being a catalyst that promotes growth within each member of your organization through establishing clear goals, and (2) by seeing that they receive the training they need to succeed?
5. When considering the purchase of new tools, how can you clarify the factors involved with the decision? Will you work through the process suggested in this chapter?

# REINFORCED BY CLEAR EXPECTATIONS

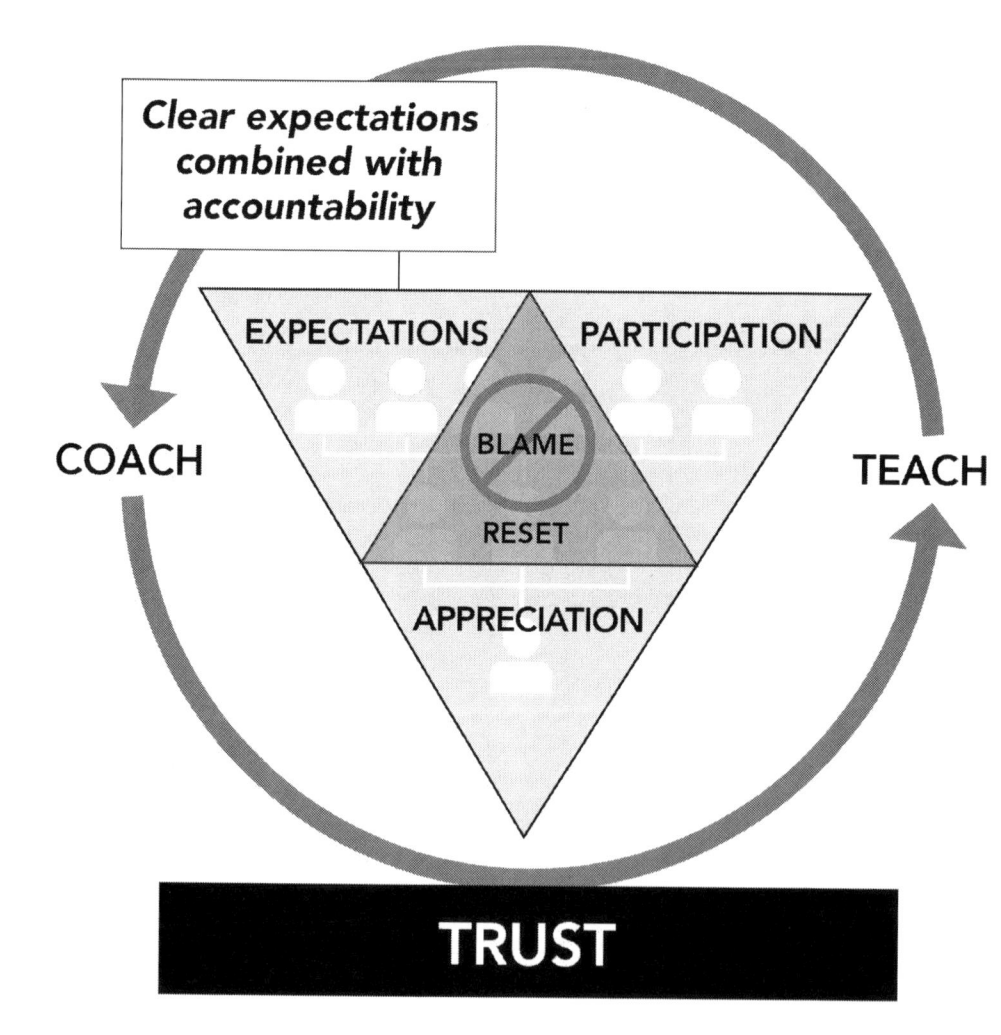

*Clear expectations combined with accountability*

COACH

EXPECTATIONS

PARTICIPATION

BLAME

RESET

APPRECIATION

TEACH

**TRUST**

CHAPTER EIGHT

# The Power of Clear Expectations, Coupled with Accountability

*Lesson: Leaders expect the best from their teams, and then lead the way.*

Standing beside a gorgeous mountain lake one afternoon, I was attached to a parasail anticipating being airborne within seconds. My neighbor and expert boater, Doug Hadley, had invited my family to spend the day parasailing behind his ski boat. As the evening sun began to dip behind the cliffs that surrounded the lake, it was finally my turn. My sons were on either side of me, keeping the sides of the chute open, and the boat was slowly making its way forward in the water.

All three of my teenage sons had already been up and had a blast. After my last son landed gently on the beach, Doug brought the boat around so I could climb out and to get harnessed up. Just before stepping out of the boat, I heard Doug yell to me: "Bob, if anything happens to you while you are getting up, get your feet in front of you and keep them there."

By way of background, when first arriving at the lake, we had a tutorial on parasailing. We found there was a critical element to ensure a rider's safety. Before launching, the rope that connected the boat to the rider had to be carefully snaked across the beach in large

S shape curves with no overlapping. Nothing was to be between the boat and the rider. Once we were ready, Doug would slowly drive the boat out into the water at about 5 miles per hour. At the exact moment, the boat and the line attached to the rider were completely tight and off the sand, he would gun the throttle and, like magic, the chute would go up in the air with an excited passenger dangling beneath. We also discovered this wasn't like holding on to a ski rope—you couldn't simply let go and be released. Riders had a full body harness around their entire upper torso so they were fully committed to the process.

I now heard the boat begin to gain speed and prepared for liftoff. This being my first time ever parasailing, I didn't know what to expect other than to enjoy the thrill ride my sons had raved about. Ready, set ... and suddenly, instead of being forty or fifty feet in the air, I was fifteen feet underwater while the boat kept increasing its speed. I felt desperate—the water moving faster and faster beside me, my body submerging ever deeper, seemingly sinking like a rock. I remembered Doug's instructions and struggled to position my feet in front of me while squeezing my eyes shut so my contact lenses wouldn't get ripped out.

Now, in that moment I knew three things. The first is I was totally committed to this experience. There was no choice other than to go with it—I was quite literally hooked in. Second, surprisingly I felt no fear. I completely trusted my neighbor. He is still the best boater that I know ... and if he wasn't worried, I wasn't worried. Finally, I had to do all I could to keep my feet in front of me. Those final words of advice were what I was hanging onto with all my might.

With my mind focusing on these thoughts and the water swirling past my body, just as quickly as I was submerged I popped out of the water like a cork. Within seconds, I was in the air—first twenty, then forty then eighty feet above the water, experiencing an unforgettable ride.

**Clarity Overcomes Chaos**

Clarity not only kept chaos from becoming a catastrophe; it was the catalyst to an amazing experience. The clarity in that moment of knowing that I was committed, knowing that I trusted Doug, and knowing what to do turned everything around. Indeed, clarity is power—and few things are more powerful than clear, unambiguous expectations. The expectation Doug set of what to do if things went wrong made all the difference in the world between a tragedy and a once-in-a-lifetime experience. The word "expect" comes from the Latin verb *expectare*, which means "to look out." With the mental map he gave me, I was able to "look out" and know exactly what to do right when I needed to take action.

This power of clarity was especially game changing during the period of chaos I stepped into at PageNet. As we discussed earlier, the company's unprecedented growth, labor intensive systems, inadequate physical facilities, and a weak management team had created the perfect storm. But the clarity that had come from solving similar challenges in the past, along with a clear vision of what was possible and where the business was heading, made the pathway ahead well defined. The needs and expectations were clear.

**Clear Expectations = a Win for Everyone**

Clear expectations are critical within every part of an organization: for the group as a whole, for the individual employee, and also for the leader. When they are well thought out, with clear communication and buy-in everyone wins. First, for an organization, few things can compare with the power of an entire group being in full alignment and agreement over how every member of the team contributes to the success of the whole and what that success looks like. Next, clear expectations allow individual team members to understand, and own, their personal contribution to the organization's success. Finally, when leaders have thoughtfully defined expectations for their team, they have an internal guidance system and framework that enables them to lead, in part, through intuition. Certainly, the process of establishing clear expectations for oneself is at the heart of a leader's responsibilities—it is a task as important as laying out expectations out for the organization.

What then is the process of establishing expectations for team members? It begins with a clearly defined vision and mission, as discussed in chapter 5. But an owner's vision for the organization is just the start. "Micro-vision" for each team member is then needed, and that is what clear expectations provide. To achieve this, for decades many business leaders defaulted to "job descriptions"—detailed statements of most elements to a position, with just the right touch of legalese to stand up in court if the need ever occurred. Job descriptions, however, are far too one dimensional to serve as personal vision statements for team members; they provide no context to the position, give no sense of priority, and certainly don't describe what success look like. In fact, they are a really poor tool for setting expectations. They may have a place from a risk management standpoint, but they don't from a leadership perspective.

**Roles, Goals, and Metrics**

Instead of relying on job descriptions for setting expectations, I have seen great success in using a process Stephen Covey described years ago: defining roles and goals, and then (using my language) establishing success metrics—numeric indicators that let us all know what success looks like. As the clear expectations from roles and goals allow us to "look out" and see the impact of a team member's contribution, then the final form of vision is knowing how we will measure success through targeted metrics.

The phrase "roles and goals" may be new, but the process of setting them is likely familiar and is very straightforward. A well-defined role describes one of the many "hats" a team member wears throughout the day. Defining this begins with a leader working through the roles a team member has, using only his or her intuition to define those roles. To be effective, a team member should not have more than five to seven defined roles. After identifying the team member's role, the leader then concisely captures or describes each role with a word or two, while ensuring that the words used have meaning and context to them. Some roles may need to be folded into others. But once this exercise is finished, these defined roles create a multi-dimensional picture of a team member's contribution.

**A Multistep Process**

Now, let me say at the onset, it seems opposite to the model that in an upside-down organization the process of defining roles, goals, and metrics starts with the leader. You might ask, isn't that using the "top-down" approach? It would be if it stopped at the leadership level and was then passed onto each team member with no discussion or input from the team member. To the contrary, this is an iterative process that starts with the leader and then brings in the team member. Finally, the two of them working *together* create the final product and establish the team member's immediate and long-term goals.

It is key, however, for the process to begin with the leader because achieving this initial clarity of heart and mind allows the leader to then facilitate discussions with each team member in a very positive way. You can't help create outside of you what you haven't begun to build inside of you. Further, establishing a vision for each team member builds confidence within a leader as his or her intuition is sharpened and how things are supposed to "feel" is cemented deeper inside.

**Emotive Words and Phrases**

In starting the process of defining roles, I recommend using *emotive* words that grab the heart and inspire. A billing clerk, for instance, may have a role of "collector"—or the more powerful role of a "revenue champion." A salesperson could have a role of "sales associate"—or the more accurate role of a "customer advocate." A great role description gives life to the individual responsibility and quickly conveys the outcome wanted more than the actions needed to get there. Recently, I was working with a client and asking him to define his own roles as a practitioner in his dental office. The two he arrived at for himself were "dentist" and "boss." I explained that those were a great start but that the words focused on the "functions" he did rather than the endpoint he was seeking. After ten minutes of discussion, he came up with two new descriptors for his roles: "life changer" and "coach." And with the added dimensions of these titles, the goals and metrics that flow out of them will be completely different.

**Goals and Metrics**

With the roles well defined using outcome-oriented, emotive words, leaders then continue their homework by asking: what are the goals for each of those roles? Brainstorming and thinking out loud are called for here—and this takes time. Whiteboards can be an effective way to capture thoughts for this work. Excel spreadsheets can also prove helpful. Plain old legal pads do as well. Whatever the methodology you choose, what's important is to put the details in writing so they are specific, clear, and something that can be revisited. Each role should have very specific, but not an overwhelming number of, goals. Two to three goals per role is about right.

Finally, defining the goals then leads to asking: for this goal, how will we know we've achieved it? Not every goal will have a number associated with its success, but a metric is a numeric indicator of success. Like the scoreboard at a sporting event, metrics serve as the culminating measure of all the work that has taken place on the field. While metrics do not measure everything, they do measure something ... and that something can be very valuable. As Dennis Webb taught, numbers tell a story—and it is the story that is so valuable by tracking key metrics. When a wisely chosen metric is achieved, it represents significant work and effort. When it is missed, it begs the question "why?"—and that question is instrumental in finding ways to nail the metric the next time. Some goals and metrics will encompass more than one goal, and they become the benchmark that allows the organization to gauge success over time.

### Setting Goals and Defining Metrics

I find it very helpful to define each step sequentially, first doing roles, then goals, and finally metrics. The words used in the roles become the source of inspiration for the goals, and the roles and goals together help establish the metrics.

An example from a client might be illustrative. We had been working through the roles and goals of her team, and the last we focused on was her office manager. My client defined six roles for this team member, including financial steward, patient care champion, HR coordinator, and IT liaison. With these four roles in mind, a sampling of her goals looked like this:

1. Financial steward—account for the practice timely, accurately, and efficiently; ensure that funds are handled using internal controls and with complete integrity.
2. Patient care champion—create relationships of genuine trust and confidence with each patient; assist patients in understanding the need for treatment, converting that need into a desire.
3. HR coordinator—hire and keep the right team members, motivating and rewarding them for exceptional results, fostering true ownership and teamwork.

4. IT liaison—ensure system is secure, consistently backed up, and reliable.

From these goals then naturally flow the metrics for each:
1. Financial steward—books are reconciled by the fifth day of the next month and accounts receivable is less than one month's collections.
2. Patient care champion—treatment acceptance by patients is 80 percent or higher, and appointment cancellations are less than 5 percent.
3. HR coordinator—one-on-ones are scheduled and conducted with every team member at least every four months.
4. IT liaison—system is backed up nightly, and downtime is zero while screen refresh time is less than a second.

It may seem like a large mountain to climb to do this, but once you begin, the process really makes sense. If it feels hard, go back to clarifying the roles, and don't move onto the next step until the step you are on feels right and makes sense. The more time you spend on each step, the easier the process becomes.

**The Next Step**

With this heavy lifting completed, the next step in this process is meeting with each team member individually. This may take more than one session, as the leader shares the work he or she has done so far and reviews the person's roles, goals, and metrics as currently defined. The leader then invites the team member to help refine and change this work as needed—eventually creating a set of roles, goals, and metrics that *both* the leader and team member are satisfied with. It is an investment of time doing this, but few things yield higher returns than creating genuine clarity for both the leader and the team member regarding expectations.

## Rolling These Out

Once the work is done at the individual level, getting buy in from the team is the last step—and it is vital that this be done right. An all-team meeting is held where everyone has the chance to share their respective roles, goals, and metrics. Questions are answered, discussion unfolds, and ultimately agreements are made that form the basis for everything moving forward. This can be a very powerful team meeting when the ambiguity of the past is left in the rearview mirror, while the team formally hits the reset button with new clarity, commitment, and agreement.

The power of being on the same page for an organization is profound. It leads to a sense of unity, synergy, and harmony. In addition, one of the direct benefits of clearly defining roles, goals, and metrics is eliminating a source of conflict within an organization. I have repeatedly found, as my good friend Travis Anderson taught me, that conflict in business happens most often because of unclear roles, goals, and expectations. Such lack of clarity leads to unclear boundaries, unclear ownership, and a lack of engagement by team members. Conflict becomes part of the culture, and rather than being able to focus on the competition from without, more and more time is devoted to competition from within. Clear expectations help eliminate this dynamic.

## Adapting for Larger Organizations

This process sounds doable for a small business...but what about a larger one? How can it work when there are fifty, or five hundred, or five thousand employees? The secret is to keep it at the individual team member level. The person who is the point of accountability for that team member is the "leader" who begins the process and, in the end, facilitates the outcome with the employee. It needs to be this way, because roles and goals then become the basis for the team member coaching that occurs on a one-on-one level.

### Aligning New Team Members

When new team members are brought on board, setting expectations needs to happen very early. Without this clarity, and the associated commitment from their leader to teach and train them so they have the tools to meet the expectations, team members become confused and disengaged. They then are more prone to fall into the trap of poor performance, inefficient processes, and frequent conflict—all indicators of unclear expectations. This becomes a losing proposition for the entire organization, especially the leader who is relying on them to help the team succeed.

If Doug Hadley would not have set clear expectations for me when I got off the boat, the results would have been very different when I was pulled underwater. I shudder to think what might have happened—and how he would have felt personally responsible for it. Instead, it's a great story, and one we laugh about often.

What to do then? Use new team members' job-specific roles, goals, and metrics as a training document. Bring it out in the interview, use it on the first day of the job, and continue to refer to it thereafter. Establish specific goals from it that are understandable and achievable, and lay out a road map for new employees that show all they need to master to be perfect for the job. As new team members experience their learning curve, begin to set new goals—and allow the roles and goals to transition from a training document to a coaching document that will be consistently used in goal setting and in their daily job performance.

**Accountability Becomes Natural Now**

The final win from defining roles, goals, and metrics is that you put ambiguity out to pasture, and as my colleague Kevin Miller describes it, a leader can create a "cadence of accountability." Accountability is all too often viewed as a negative because of uncertainty. Wouldn't it be wonderful to make accountability natural, simple, positive, and maybe even easy? Few things are more conflicted and stressful for a leader than to try to hold team members accountable for their performance when the up-front expectations are unclear. Clear expectations, however, eliminate this dynamic and allow a leader to make accountability natural.

Creating an organizational cadence of accountability begins with the leader. Serving as a facilitator, the leader sees that roles, goals, and metrics are consistently followed up on both formally and informally. Follow-up is the key. Without it, accountability breaks down. But through a simple process called "return and report" where deadlines and goals are discussed one-on-one, accounted for, and further plans made—including the next return-and-report session—personal responsibility and accountability are reinforced and become part of the culture. In this way, the roles, goals, and metrics are like a map. They outline a path, allow progress to be tracked, and identify what success will look like when you arrive there. Accountability happens when we return to the map, see where we are compared to where we said we would be, and then make further plans.

### The Return-and-Report Process

To be effective, a return-and-report session needs to cover at least four things:

1. What has gone well? What are the "wins" the team member has experienced in achieving his or her goals?
2. Where are things currently compared to goal (both numeric and otherwise)? With the proper metrics in place up front, you can

compare your ideal metrics to what the metrics are saying now. If the goal was to have accounts receivable under one-month collections, and it is at one and a half months, then that needs to be discussed.
3. What does it all mean? Using the example up above—why the discrepancy? What is driving the difference between the goal and the actual?
4. What do we do next? What are the goals now to bring actuals in line with the goals? What does the employee do different going forward?

Reviewing the expectations helps make them real. Further, the focus that comes from consistently asking these four questions, and capturing the answers in writing, keeps the cadence of accountability alive.

**Who Reports to Whom?**

To clarify further, it is the team member who is returning and reporting to the leader, not the leader returning and reporting to the team member. Personal responsibility at all levels is paramount in an upside-down organization, and it is reinforced by the expectation that team members do the reporting back. The goal of accountability goes further than being accountable only to the leader. It transcends this level and then moves within the team member to accountability to the group, with final accountability to the team member themselves. This is another way upside-down leaders create leaders in their teams. Building on the foundation of trust and CARE created by upside-down leadership, clear roles, goals, and metrics allow an organization—and an owner—to create that type of accountability. Accountability is one more piece of how you create an ultra-high-performance culture, as everyone is enlisted to perform at a higher level and empowered to view his or her role as that of an owner and stakeholder.

**The Gift of Clear Expectations**

One final thought: clear expectations are a gift a leader gives to his or her team. Ambiguous expectations, unclear targets, and undefined roles create individual confusion, contention, and disengagement for team members. Set well, clear expectations mean your team will not encounter these signs of organizational malaise.

Roles, goals, and metrics are also a gift leaders give themselves. Sad but true, so often I hear a business owner say: "I really don't know what my people do." Yes, it takes time to achieve the level of clarity I've been describing in this chapter—but the power of clarity to a leader is immense. If expectations are unclear in the leader's mind, how can they be clear in anyone else's? When they are not, chaos will abound. But, as I experienced the day I went parasailing, with clear expectations, follow-up, and a cadence of accountability, the chaos will be driven out as the group is in full alignment.

**Coach's Challenge**

1. Over the next week, could you develop five to seven clear and defined roles that give life and meaning to each part your team members play?
2. After arriving at roles, can you devote an hour to coming up with two to three goals for every role each team member has?
3. Next, how could you develop a metric or numeric indicator to measure success or progress? Will you do what it takes to do this?
4. Will you meet with each team member, and then with the whole team, to discuss the roles, goals, and metrics of each individual?
5. How can you schedule times to follow up with each team member regularly to discuss, evaluate, and adjust roles and goals so everybody is held accountable for their work?

## LEADS TO A CULTURE OF GENUINE PARTICIPATION

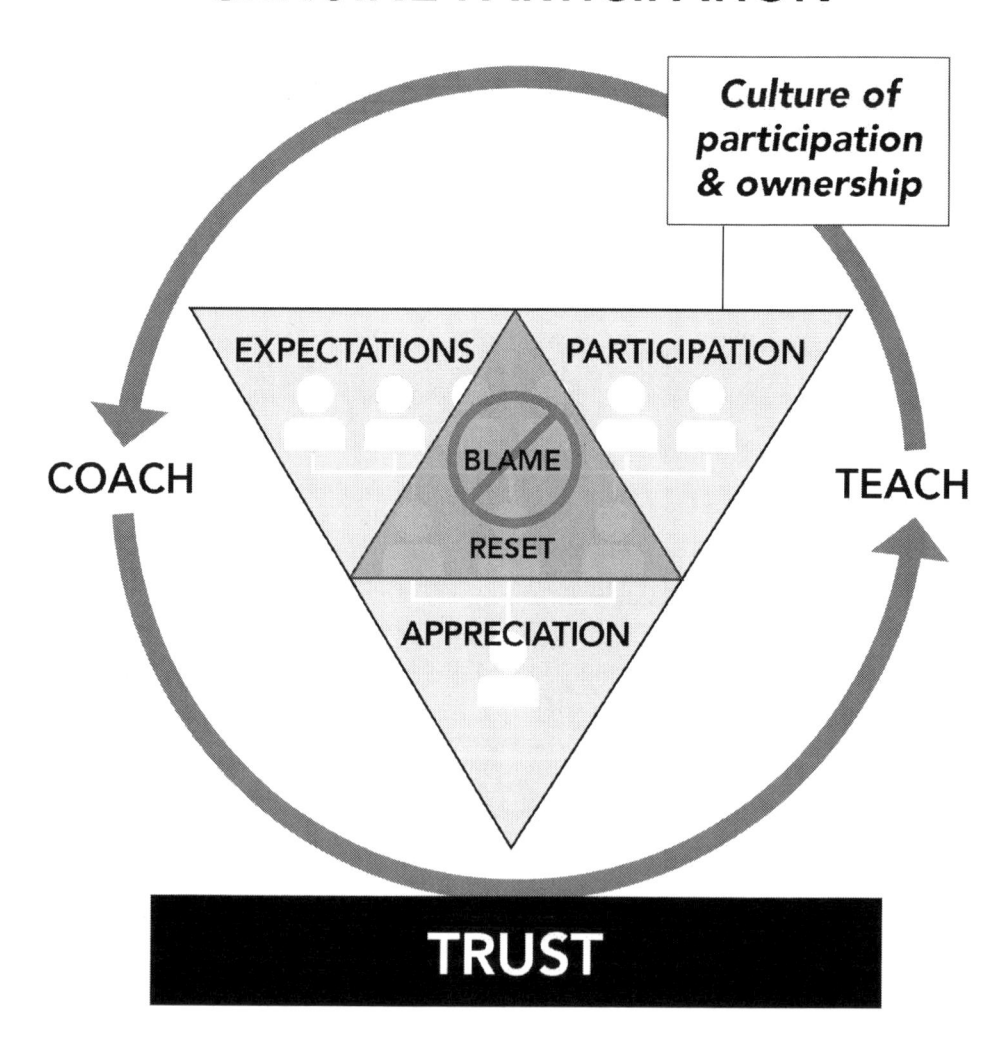

*Culture of participation & ownership*

COACH

TEACH

EXPECTATIONS

PARTICIPATION

BLAME

RESET

APPRECIATION

**TRUST**

CHAPTER NINE

# Creating a Culture of Participation and Ownership

*Lesson: Leaders know that participation breeds ownership, commitment, and results.*

With clear expectations and accountability in place, what's next? What is the next action an owner takes to truly turn an organization upside down and in a wholly different direction? How do you build an effective and efficient team of owners, of genuine stakeholders who care almost as deeply as those who signed the operating agreement and have the debt on the business team? By establishing a culture of genuine involvement and participation in decision making regarding goals, processes, and *especially* problem solving. This fosters ownership of both issues and performance. It is another way that effective leaders get out of the way and make their teams high performing.

To illustrate this simple principle, and its profound impact, let me share with you a conversation I had with a gentleman on a plane a few years ago. I found that he was working for Toyota Motor Company in San Antonio, Texas, building the new Toyota Camry in their south Texas plant. Since I had worked for Ford Motor Company right out of business school for a couple of years, hearing of his job piqued my interest.

We started asking each other questions. He was a tall, friendly, gregarious individual, and it soon became evident that he possessed a great sense of pride in his work. His 20 year old son was sitting next to him on the plane, and you could tell this father felt he was doing something important. During our visit, I discovered that this father also worked for General Motors in California for over fifteen years before joining Toyota and had only recently relocated his family to Texas, where he worked at this new plant.

As the flight continued and we got deeper into our discussion, I leaned over and looked him in the eyes. Cutting to the chase, I simply asked the question I was wondering about: "So now that you've experienced both companies, can you tell me what the difference is between GM and Toyota?" He thought for a moment, and then without hesitation replied, "Bob, it's really simple." And then staring off in the space of the cabin, he said with a sense of sadness, "At GM, we had a ratio of one engineer for every five line workers. When a change needed to take place on our production line, the engineer would come and tell us what was going to change." Then he said something I will never forget. He turned to me with a smile that revealed great confidence and pride, and said, "At Toyota, however, we have one engineer for twenty-five line workers. There, when a change needs to take place, the engineers come down, we have a meeting, and we all talk about it. The guys and gals on the line are viewed as the experts, and we have not only a voice at the table—but we have a critical voice at the table where collectively all of us arrive at a solution."

**Contrasting Two Leadership Styles**

There is no better description I can think of to contrast the two leadership styles and how they either invest or disinvest people in an organization. My new friend clearly was enormously proud of the work that he was doing at Toyota, while GM sadly was now simply a memory. Frankly, though, I was not surprised by his comments. I personally believe Toyota to be one of the finest companies in the world, and one of the few organizations that transformed itself by fully implementing, and then building on, the cultural and operational teachings of W. Edwards Deming – the father of modern quality improvement paradigms. A company like GM, however, has employed the top-down management style for more than a century, believing that control is the final goal within an organization believing with control you get predictable (if not lackluster) results.

**The Myth of Control**

Control, however, is a myth. Let me repeat that because it is one of the key take homes of this book and paradigms for a leader to accept: Control is a myth. As my colleague Kevin Miller shared with me, there are four components to the human personality: the heart, the mind, the body, and the spirit. But there is only one that is controlled at work ... and that is the body. All the rest are completely *volunteered*. The goal of an upside-down leader and organization is not control; it is ownership because ownership creates not just satisfactory results, but outstanding results. It also establishes an amazing sense of fulfillment in team members. Just as I could see pride in the face of my friend sitting next to me, ownership places that same sense of pride within team members, and that pride becomes one of the greatest assets an organization has. Individuals who feel respected, valued, and listened to will invest their heart into a business—and consistently do very high-quality work. As Stephen Covey once said, "You can buy a man's back, but you can't buy their heart—they give it to you." A culture of participation is a fundamental element in getting your team to throw themselves in totally, heart and back combined.

**From Directing to Facilitating**

To make this happen—to create a culture of participation and ownership—leaders must, once again, flip their focus. They must step back from the traditional role of boss or director to seeing themselves more as a facilitator. Then, when a new problem emerges, an effective facilitator keeps the team focused on the topic at hand without dominating the discussion. They have learned to listen very well and resist the urge to jump in and throw their own ideas out first. They have also internalized the importance of giving everyone a respected voice. You foster this type of environment by realizing your job is to ask the right questions, and then help the group find the answer by keeping the end in mind. An upside-down leader recognizes team members have a valuable perspective and their insights may indeed be key to finding the right solution—and the right solution is the goal, not the ego-driven "I'm always right" solution that is characteristic of (actually) weak and insecure leaders.

This critical facilitative role is why I also call upside-down leadership transfacilitative leadership ™. Rather than the traditional role of telling and directing, wise leaders act as a catalyst to help their team ask the right questions and collectively arrive at an effective solution. Except in a time of crisis, leaders should not be the group "rescuer" ensuring everything is done "one way and one way only." That's command-and-control style leadership, and while it creates compliance in the short run, it establishes resentment and noncompliance in the long run.

Dennis Webb offered an amazing example of this facilitative style when I worked with him at Franklin Covey. He was a natural facilitator and he wanted disagreement in his meetings. He felt that if everyone was on the same page immediately, something was being missed. Sometimes, he would even ask an individual to take the role of what was called the black hat. This person was charged with disagreeing with where the group was going by asking counter questions: the questions that weren't being put on the table. Dennis would spread a deck of cards on the table, and the first person who pulled out a black card took on the job of the antagonist—the one who wasn't going along with the crowd. That type of environment fostered a level of mental and emotional excellence because as a management team working under Dennis, we knew everyone had a voice.

We also knew that he was very committed to the process of having us collectively arrive at a solution. And when a group arrives at a solution and is committed to it, the group owns what that outcome is going to be and the steps required to get there. In the *Seven Habits of Highly Effective People*, Stephen Covey said, "Without involvement, there is no commitment. Mark it down, asterisk it, circle it, underline it. No involvement, no commitment." Dennis was a living example of this practice.

**The Questions Are the Answer**

One final thought is when we are young and just leaving school, it seems knowing the right answer is the greatest outcome from knowledge. The longer I live, though, the more I realize that the purpose of any type of education is not to provide the right answers, but to teach students how to ask the right questions—because, as mentioned earlier, the questions are the answer. And, the better the questions, the better the outcome and results. Therefore, a fundamental role of an upside-down leader is to ensure the right questions are being asked. The Level Five Leaders Jim Collins describes in Good to Great (see chapter 2) were excellent at asking the right questions. Those questions evoked lively discussion, conclusion, focus, and finally ownership.

### Facilitating Discussions

When facilitating a discussion with a team either (1) solving a problem or (2) refining a system a few standard questions can ramp up the discussion quickly. Before anything is discussed, the opening step is to clearly define the goal. In other words, "What is the goal of this process or system?" Or, "What is the goal of this discussion?"

It is important to capture this in writing and ensure everyone can see the statement that comes from this first part of the discussion. To make that happen, write the goal on a large three-by-four-foot Post-it Note flip-chart pad (available at office supply stores) or on a whiteboard, if one is available. Whiteboards are great tools to focus attention and capture discussion points. The point is, virtually any room can become a conference room. Just use whatever is available to guarantee that all can see the goal.

Next, with that clear outcome in mind, the team is asked to capture what is working *toward* that goal. In other words, "What are we doing today that is leading us toward achieving this goal?" This doesn't need to be an exhaustive list, but certainly comprehensive.

Once that discussion has concluded, the next question is: "What is *not* working toward that goal?" And, as the "not working" list is compiled, be sure to capture those points as well—and to complete this section before solutions are discussed.

Once what is working and not working is spelled out, it can be exciting to see the solutions that arise from this level of clarity. And if the group gets stuck on finding a solution, asking the question "Why?" three or four times about something that is not working can unfreeze the group. The goal of this is to sort out and find root causes for the chronic issues that can weaken a business—and turn them into strengths instead.

**Eliciting Participation**

Simple things can be done to help elicit participation from all team members in these kinds of discussions. Post-it Notes are an amazing tool to place in the hands of each member of a group—even in gatherings up to 200. The Post-its allow individuals to capture their answers to the question being presented. One note per answer allows for a quick summation of their replies. These notes are then placed on the easel-size Post-its, a whiteboard, or even a window. They can either be read individually or grouped into "word clouds." Displaying them gives you a very quick way to see the group members' ideas, suggestions, and overall mindset. This is taking the concept of "seek first to understand" and putting it into a group setting.

**The Leader's Voice and Capturing What Is Next**

There is another side to seeking first to understand, and that is to then be understood. The engineers at Toyota are not ignored in the discussion. They have a critical perspective to teach and to share. In like manner, a leader and owner has a voice in facilitative discussions, but that voice is most effective when, instead of directing, is focused on asking questions such as, "Have we thought about this?" or "Have we considered the impact that this decision might have?"

A fundamental step throughout this discussion is capturing the resulting decisions as well as the follow-up items with specific goals, assignments, and due dates. Next, those goals, assignments, and due dates must be followed up on to close the loop and track the success of the intended changes. Otherwise, there is no point for the discussion and the opposite of positive change happens: buy in diminishes because the phenomena of "we always talk about the same things" take place. We change this dynamic by consistent follow-up and accountability to self and to the group. This gives a group the traction to keep moving forward. Without this, it's like driving in a car without road signs, a map, or a gas gauge. You have no clue where you are, you have no idea where you are going, and you don't know what's taking place right now or when you will come to a halt—and everyone is frustrated.

## Fostering a Culture of Participation and Ownership

What does creating a culture of participation and ownership ultimately do for a leader? It is one more means of getting out of the way so the team will be engaged, own the process, and create the desired results. How is it that Toyota is one of the greatest auto companies in the world and consistently builds automobiles for a lower cost and higher quality than almost any other auto company out there? Because they have created this form of group facilitation, ownership, buy in, and implementation. They have fostered a culture that consists of what every small business owner or leader can do as well:

- *instead of directing—asking*
- *instead of telling—promoting*
- *instead of controlling—facilitating*

Getting things done may seem slower at first and it does take time up front. But, oh, how it saves time in the end and produces extraordinary results. And the win for leaders in an upside-down organization is that creating a culture of participation dramatically reduces the load on themselves—while allowing them to continue to focus on their highest and best purpose.

## Coach's Challenge

1. How could you flip your focus to become more of a facilitator who asks the right questions and helps everybody keep the end goal in mind? Do you see the value of this move and how it will benefit your organization?
2. In what ways could you put forward your best effort to ask questions that generate discussion, conclusion, focus, and ownership?

3. Will you work to develop an atmosphere of participation in discussions, whether that is by using tools such as a white board or sticky notes, or through some other method so that a sense of ownership and pride can grow within every team member?
4. How can you ensure that decisions made from discussion are written out and understood by each team member? What will allow you to later be able to follow up on established goals, assignments, due dates, and other orders of business?

# APPRECIATION & RECOGNITION KEEP THE MAGIC GOING:

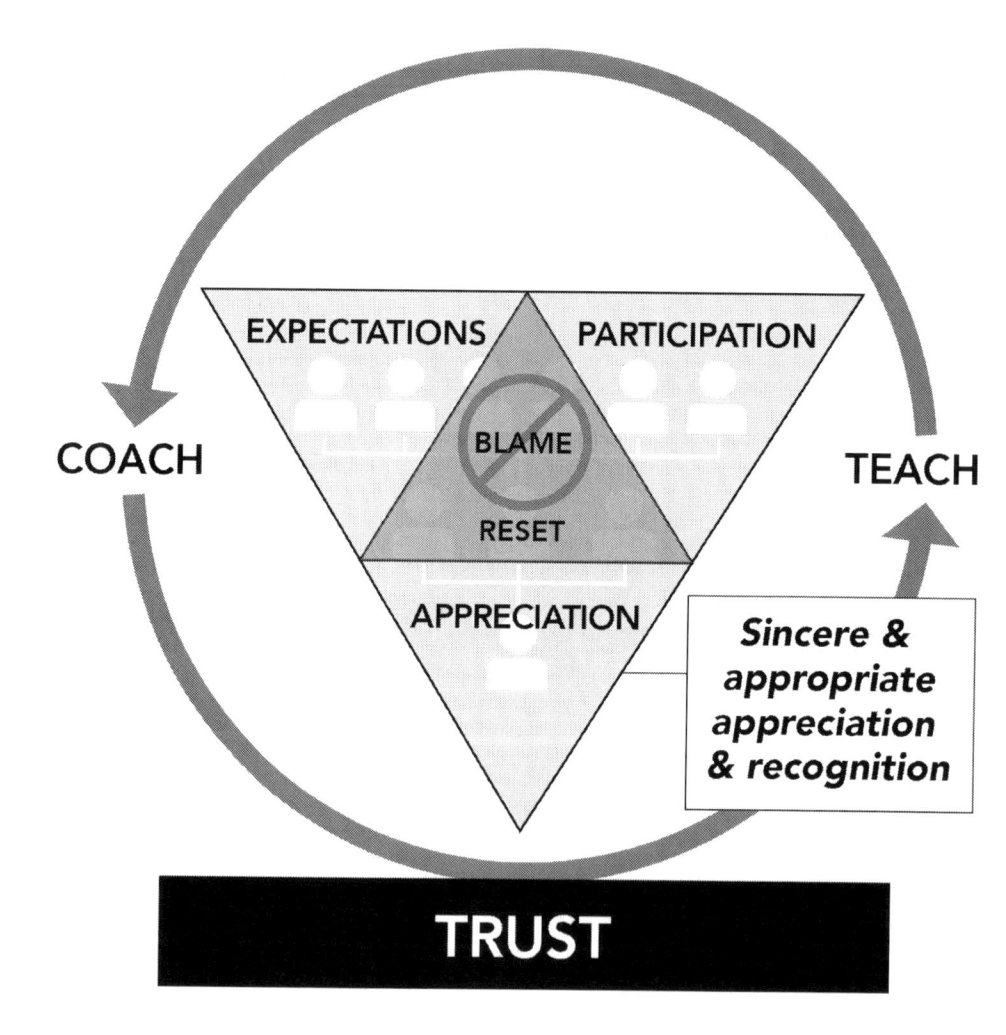

COACH

TEACH

EXPECTATIONS · PARTICIPATION

BLAME

RESET

APPRECIATION

*Sincere & appropriate appreciation & recognition*

**TRUST**

CHAPTER TEN

# What Keeps the Magic Going— Appreciation and Recognition

*Lesson: People who feel appreciated will consistently go above and beyond expectations.*

Over twenty years ago, while working at Franklin Covey, my manager Dennis Webb urgently asked a colleague and me to compile a budget for all his operating entities. At Franklin, budgets prior to this had been put together at the accounting level. Now, however, budgets were going to be compiled at the divisional level and Dennis needed help getting this done. There was a fourteen-day deadline that had to be beat, and it had to be done right. We spent the next two weeks compiling in spreadsheet form the operating budgets for every one of Dennis's five operating divisions. I had a few years of experience at other companies doing this, including Ford Motor Company, and Mike was a brilliant analyst. Together we made a great team and nailed the deadline.

Yet, this process was long and included twelve- to fourteen-hour days compiling, questioning, analyzing, and compiling again. When everyone else left the building, Mike and I were still there. Dennis was the sort of leader who empowered us with such confidence and direction that we wanted to create something that not only would make him proud, but would be a model for the company itself.

When the project was completed, and after we presented our project to Dennis, Mike and I went back to our normal roles as an operations director and a lead IT tech. There was a real sense of accomplishment from the project and we were proud of the work that had been done, but now it was back to "normal." The next day in both of our in-boxes, however, was a card. Our cards included a heartfelt note from Dennis expressing his appreciation for the work we had done and the professional way we had done it. He had also enclosed a gift certificate to the nicest restaurant in Salt Lake City at the time: the Chart House.

This was totally unexpected and absolutely appreciated. Mike and I had not done this work anticipating any sort of reward. We were simply following through with the loyalty that Dennis had fostered within us. His leadership style had created such a real sense of ownership and pride, we didn't think twice about taking on this assignment. But when he reciprocated that loyalty with his own gesture of gratitude and appreciation, the bond between us became welded even stronger.

How long did it take Dennis Webb to write two cards and have two gift certificates on hand? I imagine the cards took as much as five minutes each and his secretary, Jeannie, likely picked up the gift certificates on her way home from the office the night before. Yet, twenty-five years later, the impact of those five minutes for Dennis and half an hour for Jeannie is still felt. Truly, people remember the unexpected.

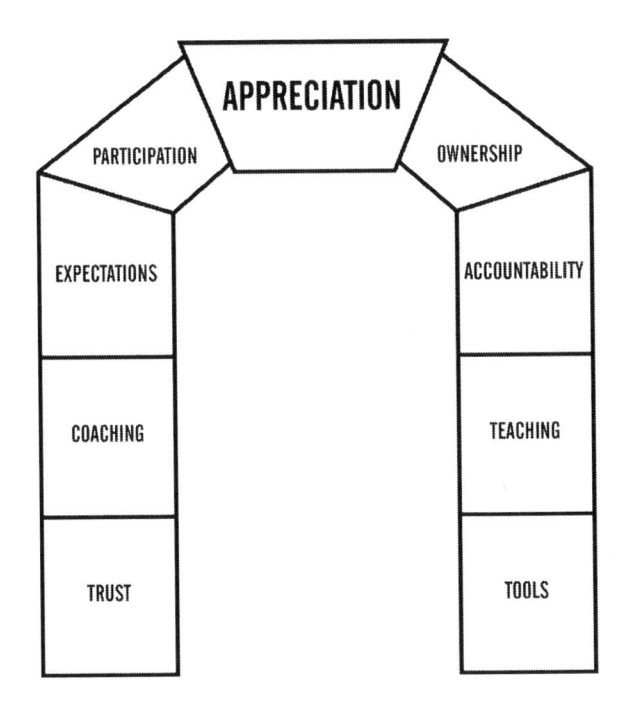

```
                    APPRECIATION
        PARTICIPATION        OWNERSHIP

        EXPECTATIONS         ACCOUNTABILITY

        COACHING             TEACHING

        TRUST                TOOLS
```

**The Keystone of Appreciation**

Mastering the art of leadership is much like building an arch. Every arch is built upon foundation stones and then it continues upwards into the sky. You need to start with the stones of trust and clear expectations, and from there put in place training and tools, ownership and empowerment, participation and buy in. But every arch has a keystone—the center stone at the very top that holds the whole structure together. The keystone of leadership is sincere, appropriate appreciation and recognition.

Appreciation is something that is sorely needed in business, and sorely lacking. I believe more employees quit because of a lack of recognition and appreciation than any other reason. And for something that takes such little time to do, the impact it creates upon our teams and upon ourselves is profound. Years ago, the U.S. Chamber of Commerce conducted a study to determine the overriding motivators and needs of the American worker. Surprisingly, the number one motivator was not money. Money itself is a hygiene factor. We never get enough of it and we are always capable of spending more than we have. Pay, if it is fair, is a short-term motivator. The number one need surfaced in this study was appreciation and gratitude. What truly cements a relationship between a leader and his or her team is genuine, appropriate, personalized recognition for a job well done. It isn't a one-size-fit-all approach. Every team member has a unique personality and may desire a slightly different form of appreciation. Yet every team member will benefit from being recognized for his or her contributions.

**Appreciation Is a Win-Win-Win**

In the work I do with various business teams across the country, I start every engagement by asking questions and interviewing employees to ascertain the strengths and weaknesses of the organization, and the strengths and weaknesses of the owner and leader. Almost without fail, appreciation is cited as a weak point, even with very competent leaders who are striving to create a positive environment. While appreciation is a business term for love, the act of saying thank you in an appropriate and a timely way is rarely done. Why? Because we don't understand the need. Often, leaders will tell me they neglect this activity because it takes time or because it isn't in their natural "makeup" to say thank you. But these are all excuses. Leaders who commit to consistently and authentically expressing "thanks," while not waiting for a "thanks" back, are providing the highest form of pay—the kind that cannot be written with a check.

Often, I demonstrate the power of this one action through a simple activity during team trainings. I pass out thank-you cards, two cards per person. Then I give them five minutes to write a sincere heartfelt note of appreciation for the team members sitting on either side of them. Once the time is up and the writing is completed, the team members are asked to hold those note cards in their hands, and then I ask this question: how do you feel right now? Much to their surprise, even before the cards are distributed, the team members feel a profound sense of pride, unity, and love within the room. The simple act of expressing genuine appreciation heightens our sense of humanity and instills within us deep feelings of gratitude, respect, loyalty, and kindness. Showing appreciation is a triple win: It's a win for the person being recognized, a win for the person doing the recognition, and, finally, a win for the entire organization.

**How to Start**

What should leaders do to make this a part of their leadership style? Begin by investing some time tomorrow to pick up a few gift certificates at your favorite restaurant. Purchase a handful of Hallmark cards. Have them available and use them when you see team members consistently going above and beyond. Frankly, the notes don't have to be written on anything formal. If necessary, you can use a Post-it Note or a piece of scratch paper. The key is to have small tokens -- things that you can give team members with your handwritten notes to convey your feelings of gratitude. What else can you do? Develop a practice of informally thanking each of your team members at the end of the day, or find a way to express your gratitude after completion of a big project. Celebrate wins as often as you can. Doing so will help you turn appreciation into a habit.

Once again, people remember the unexpected. The thank-you card and gift certificate Dennis Web gave me was unexpected. A Post-it Note on somebody's desk can be just as unexpected, as can pulling somebody in at the end of the day to simply say, "Thanks! I noticed."

**Turbocharging Appreciation**

What makes a gesture of appreciation even more impactful is when it recognizes above-and-beyond performance and then focuses on three things:

1. First, be specific about *what* the behavior you are commending. It needs to be clear what you are praising the person for.
2. Next, share in a sentence *why* the behavior you saw is so important to you and your team.
3. Finally, express *how* the person's action aligns with the core values of your organization.

These three points combined not only establish a sense of appreciation for what was done, but also clarifies how that action meets one of your specific needs. Further, using this three-step rule in showing appreciation reinforces the stated values and mission of your organization. It explains both what was so important—and why. This turbocharges appreciation into a gift that endures.

How then do you make sure that your gestures are genuine and appropriate? First, follow the rule of three that was just explained. Then, challenge yourself at least weekly—if not twice a week—to catch your team members doing something great and to take that moment to say thank you. Whether you do it in person or in writing, do it in a way that is unexpected and impactful.

### Influencing "Volunteers"

What's the shelf life of this type of leading? Twenty-five years and counting, from my perspective. Dr. Tim Clark, a friend of a friend, wrote a book called *The Leadership Test*, which is a great little read. In his book, he makes an important observation: *Leadership is a process of influencing volunteers to achieve great things*. Underline that. Highlight that. Asterisk that. And then commit it to memory. As mentioned earlier, there are four components to the human personality—the spirit, the heart, the mind, and the body, and while we bring all of these to work, but there is only one <u>controlled</u> at work. The body. All the rest are *volunteered*. Genuine appreciation and recognition fuels the heart and enlists volunteers to do more and be more. And, as the late H. J. Heinz put it, *the best businesses run on heart power.*

Appreciation and recognition put fuel into the soul and keeps the magic going. Indeed, I have found team members who feel appreciated consistently outperform expectations. They want to, because it feels so good to work with and for a leader who recognizes and affirms their contribution, has given them ownership of their work, and is vested in the success of each member of the team.

**A Challenge**

Would you like to begin to improve your leadership tomorrow? Would you like to start making an impact on the lives and hearts of your team? Would you like to take one idea from this book, make it yours, and use it immediately? Let it be this: appropriate appreciation. Unlike building an arch, you don't have to wait for the other foundation stones to be set in place to put this keystone where it rightfully belongs. You can begin tomorrow by showing gratitude for what was done today. It might surprise people, they might wonder what you are up to, but just keep going. If needed, tell your team that you want to raise your leadership game and that you recognize this area has been a blind side. Let the people who work for you know how much you truly value their contribution. Just as Dennis Webb's thank-you had a huge impact on me, your five-minute investment to say thanks, multiplied by consistent focus and attention, could produce an impact that lasts a lifetime. Even if the impact is small, appreciation will nonetheless make a significant difference when it is appropriate, well timed, genuine, and not expected. And the act of expressing gratitude will also make a significant difference in your perspective as a leader as flip your focus to the great things your team members are doing, instead of the more frequent attention paid to the "wrong" things being done. Once again, it is a triple win: for you, the team member, and the business. Experiment with it and see.

**Coach's Challenge**

1. In your next training meeting, will you give out thank-you cards for your team members to write notes of appreciation to the people sitting beside them?
2. Will you allow this to be a moment to demonstrate the power of appreciation and your commitment to making this a habit?
3. Will you pick up a few gift cards from your favorite restaurant as well as a handful of Hallmark cards that you can use to show appreciation to your employees?
4. How can you make showing appreciation to your team, on at least a weekly basis, a habitual part of your leadership style?
5. Are there others in your life outside of work who could also use a gesture of sincere appreciation? What is keeping you from expressing your gratitude to them?

CHAPTER ELEVEN

# Culture by Design: Building Something That Is Truly Sustainable

*Lesson: We create around us what is inside us.*

Years ago, I discovered the impact a single leader can have upon culture, whether for good or ill, while working as a green behind the ears MBA at Ford Motor Company. My assignment with Ford was to act as a financial analyst in the Parts and Warranty Division. They called my cohorts and me FCGs, which stood for Ford College Graduates. It made us sound like we had just rolled off the watermelon truck. We soon found that our job was to say "no."

The culture I encountered in the Ford Finance department was unique and fascinating. It had been shaped years before by a man named Ed Lundy, who had been Ford's chief financial officer from 1967 to 1979. To his credit, Lundy was responsible for bringing "discipline and accountability" to Ford, and he introduced financial forecasting as well. Yet his most profound mark was on the culture of the organization -- a mark that persisted long past his tenure. Daily, the ghost of Lundy walked the halls of Ford finance, even though I arrived at Ford twelve years after his retirement and six years after he had gone off the board of directors.

Lundy had trained all my bosses. And his way of doing things were known as Lundyisms. While no one mentioned Lundy during my orientation, it didn't take too long to realize he was *everywhere*. Many of the Ford mid-level finance managers even carried laminated Lundyism cards around in their shirt pocket. The cards, which they had received years earlier, were still in use. These defined Lundy's expectations—even down to how the word "employee" was spelled. Per company lore, back when the typewriter and paper were the only means of written communication, Lundy ordered a cost-savings analysis which found that dropping the second 'e' in the word employee would save Ford over $100,000 per year in ink and paper. So, the spelling became "employe."

Other examples of his influence included certain phrases you couldn't say. "In the future" was taboo. Instead, you had to say "going forward." And the process of analysis at Ford was more like a scientific convention than it was an actual analytical discussion. Anything being proposed had to be written out in detail, and if there happened to be a typo on that document, the analysis was wholly rejected. The rationale was that, per Lundy, if you weren't careful enough to ensure there were no inaccuracies with the spelling, how on earth could we trust the rest of your analysis?

Although Lundy retired in 1979, and passed away in 2007, his way of formatting and using language to discuss financial reporting is still used at Ford today. How could this be? Obviously, there were CFOs who came before him and others who came on board after him. Yet his mark, was the one that left indelible fingerprints on the foundation of Ford finance. Culture is the direct reflection of the primary leader's values and style. Ed Lundy created such an overwhelming presence, set of rules, reinforced expectations, enumerated values, rewarded behaviors, and training that he continued to influence with an unseen hand for decades. There were no new laminated Lundy cards floating around Ford Finance in 1992, yet they remained the unspoken rule of how we did business, how we communicated, how we made decisions, and how we carried out our roles.

**Culture Is a Mirror**

Much earlier in the book, we discussed how personal development and leadership development foster organizational development. It works this way because culture is a mirror. Culture creates this inside-out reality. It is based upon this principle I have observed repeatedly: *In life, we create around us what is inside us.* What was inside Lundy was an overt desire to control and to save money. Ford Finance became the gatekeeper of control and funds, and that role was heavily reinforced by the organization.

Building on this thought, one of my favorite quotes is from Zig Ziglar. The longer I am alive, the more I see the truth behind it:

> Life is an echo.
> What you send out,
> comes back.
> What you sow,
> you reap.
> What you give,
> you get.
> What you see in others,
> exists in you.

That echo is never more evident than in the establishment and maintenance of an organization's culture. And the best way to create a more effective organizational culture is to create a more effective you—and then to invest the time and talent to create more effective team members.

Culture is a concept that often seems fuzzy, and yet every organization has a clearly definable and very discernible culture. It simply boils down to the embodiment of the norms, values, and expectations of the organization: how we communicate and solve problems, what we focus on, and what provides our underlying motivation. And where do those norms, values, and expectations spring from? What is the root source of these critical elements of fundamental success? From my experience, in a business they spring from the primary leader or leaders.

This happens for several reasons, the first of which stems from the influence a leader has at the very beginning stages of an organization. Early on, the primary leader's fingerprints are all over an entity. On top of this is the reality that individuals choose to be in or choose to be out of a group based upon how closely their personal norms, values, and expectations align with the prevailing norms, values, and expectations of the organization. Why were the Lundyisms still in existence at Ford? Because the men and women who remained at Ford were individuals who bought into the culture. Those who didn't (like me) stayed for a while and left.

**A Telling Exit Interview**

My supervisor at Ford was a gentleman by the name of Jim Suhay. Jim was both the man who hired me and, two years later, the man who conducted my exit interview. I left Ford because the culture, as I viewed it, was ineffective and my greatest fear at the time was I would become like my bosses—that I would learn to check my brain and heart at the door and become a cog in the organizational machine.

In my exit interview, Jim said something I will never forget. While sitting in his small office with a gun-metal gray desk, an environment that felt more like I was back in the Coast Guard than in an auto company, he peered over his reading glasses, looked at me, and said, "Bob, we made a mistake in hiring you." I gasped a little and felt rather dumbfounded. After all, I was leaving. Why would he make such a statement? I had done some solid work for them. Senior management had recently approved a $35 million parts distribution center project in Atlanta because of the work I had done as a finance analyst. And yet here he was saying that hiring me had been a mistake. I was taken aback by the comment. But his follow-up phrase cleared it all up: "You worked someplace before. You know what it is like on the outside." In other words, Ford Motor Finance was so dysfunctional that if you joined expecting a functional culture due to past experience ... forget it. In their eyes, my time working with Jim Faber before earning an MBA had ruined me. Their expectations and my expectations were miles apart.

Hearing this confirmed that leaving Ford was the right decision. No, I didn't want to become sucked into the culture. No, I didn't want to become part of those who had "selected in" and then lost their individuality.

**A New Lesson in Culture**

After Ford came the next lesson in culture at Franklin Quest. Franklin had its own culture founded in the values, norms, and expectations of their leaders—at least it did for a time. The start-up, entrepreneurial culture at the company was very fast paced, empowering, familial, and dynamic. Their mission was to change lives through the concepts they taught, and that mission was adopted by all who worked there. As the company matured, however, a new CEO was brought on who created a leadership vacuum. This man didn't know how to lead, much less how to design a culture, and as the red ink began to flow his time at the helm of the company was short. Survivors of his tenure described it as "feeling like we were dancing off a cliff. No direction, but for a time we sure felt good."

This leaderless culture was succeeded by a culture founded in the values and norms of the new chief executive officer. This CEO was hired by the founders of Franklin to take the company public. He filled the cultural vacuum with the norms and values he had acquired at his prior employer—Merrill Lynch. His singular goal was to prepare the company to go public, and the path he devised to get there was the Wall Street approach. His management decisions at Franklin were based upon quarterly earnings. In response, the company's culture morphed yet again, shifting to this new set of norms, values, and expectations—this meant pumping out as much product as you can, showing a dramatic increase of the top line, reducing costs by discontinuing the focus on new seminars and new technology, and letting the future come what may.

Franklin's board was far too vested in their initial public offering to give much thought to how well this CEO aligned with the roots of their culture. Unfortunately, this final transformation from familial and entrepreneurial to all-business and all-earnings eventually led to the company's decline and end. When they stopped continually reinventing and reinvigorating their product lines, Franklin quickly lost its reputation and market appeal. And its refusal to keep up with technology left it caught flat-footed when the first Palm Pilot PDAs (personal digital assistants—another precursor to today's cell phones) arrived on the market. Survival of the company was then only possible by merging with another company—another Utah-based training and development firm Covey Leadership Center. Franklin is an example of the importance of culture—and to how neglecting culture can bring an organization from focusing on significance to mere survival. Indeed, Franklin's inattention to culture took a company that was on the path to being a billion-dollar firm and led to its being a shadow of what it once was.

**Culture by Design or Culture by Default**

Leaders have a choice. Every organization has a culture. As my good friend Travis Anderson teaches, the choice is this: culture by design or culture by default. By design, culture is viewed as a living, breathing, supremely valuable asset that begins with leadership and then spreads throughout the organization. It is then reinforced through hiring right, astute reward systems, appropriate appreciation, timely recognition, careful use of metrics, clear expectations with self-accountability, and consistent training and development.

Culture by default, on the other hand, is a culture that just happens with no thought to its future, impact, or influence. Like planting a garden but then not pulling the weeds, a culture by default soon becomes choked off, ineffective, and mission limiting—if not dead.

**The Destiny Found in Culture**

Tony Hsieh, one of the founders of Zappos, in his book *Delivering Happiness*, makes this profound statement:

*"For individuals, character is destiny. In organizations, culture is destiny."*

The corollary to this statement is that cultures are fragile. They must be understood, respected, nurtured, and protected. Zappos is a company that goes out of its way to protect its culture. Zappos knows its culture is its one and only true competitive advantage. Anyone can ship shoes and clothing with the right amount of capital to start it. But no one can replicate the Zappos culture of unparalleled customer service. The leaders at Zappos have honed in and clarified so succinctly (1) who they are, (2) why they are, and (3) who fits with them that even after going through an arduous process of hiring, they will pay a new employee to leave if, after 90 or 180 days of being on the job, it becomes evident that the employee is not a good fit. That is how jealously they guard what they know to be their greatest asset. Zappos has created a culture by design. It is reinforced through training and training and training and then with intention and skill, the company's leaders make it a part of *everything* they do.

**The Call for Development—Starting with Self**

Harvard researchers did a very insightful study a few years ago regarding this realm of culture and cultural development. Their research showed that when businesses intentionally and consistently invested in positive cultural development, they vastly exceeded comparable businesses in terms of revenue, profit, and sustainability.

This cultural development begins, once again, by flipping your focus and starting with personal leadership development—because, as these stories show, culture ultimately is a mirror image of the values, norms, and expectations of the predominant leader or leaders. That is how you create sustainable organizations. That is how you establish true excellence: through personal development that then translates into group development and cultural development. Nothing will provide a greater return on investment—because culture is destiny, pure and simple.

**Coach's Challenge**

1. Has the culture in your business been developed more by default than by design? How could that change starting now?
2. What kind of first impressions might your clients gather from your business? Are these the impressions you would want your clients to have?
3. What would your culture need to look like for it to be a true competitive advantage? What would need to change to make that happen?
4. What will you do to influence the culture you leave behind in your business?

# THE UNSELFISH ORGANIZATION

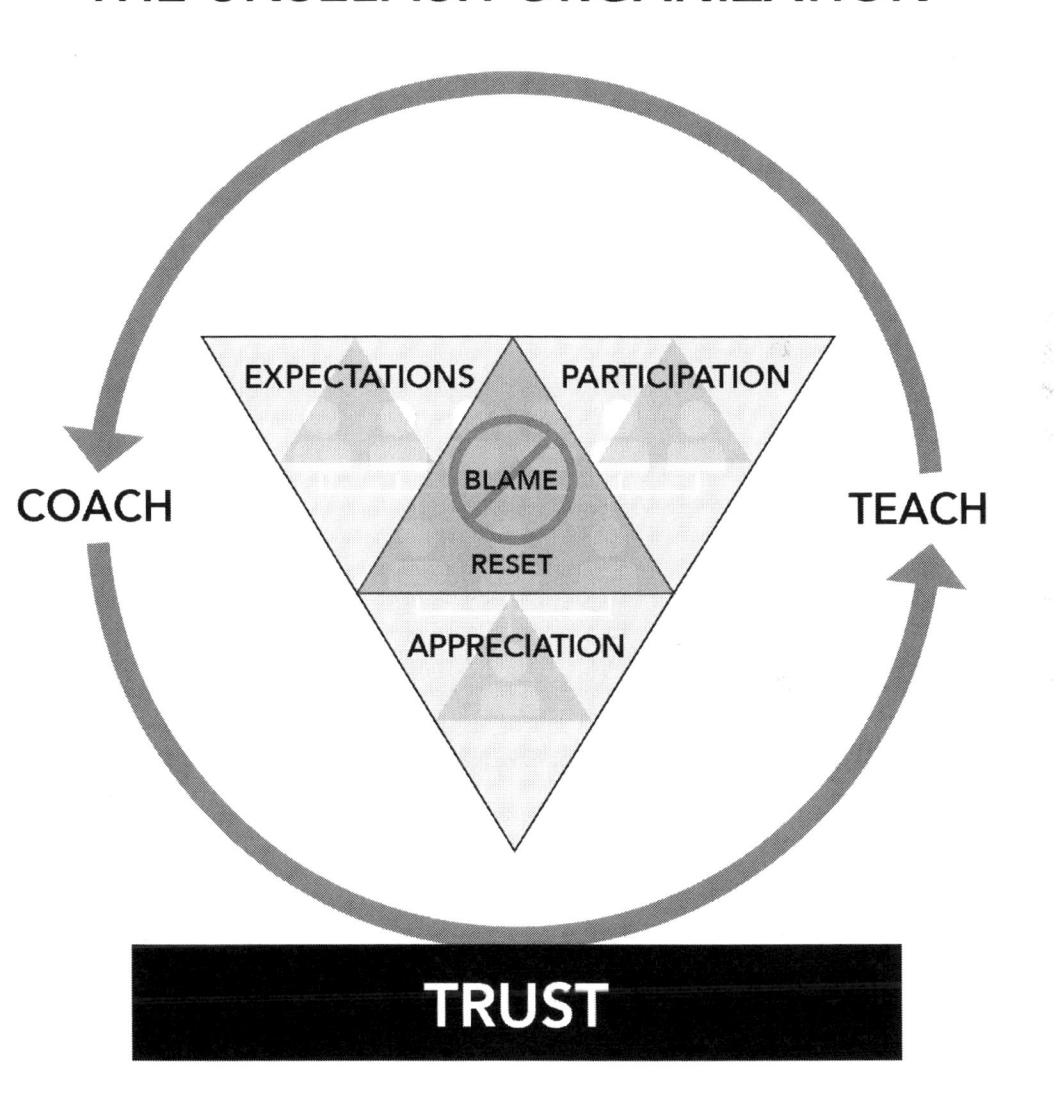

COACH

EXPECTATIONS
PARTICIPATION
BLAME
RESET
APPRECIATION

TEACH

**TRUST**

CHAPTER TWELVE

# The Unselfish Organization: What Does Ultimate Success Look Like?

*Lesson: Teamwork is just the beginning.*

In chapter 3, I shared the story of the Hillcrest Knights football team and the remarkable turnaround they experienced with a change in team leadership. I never tire of telling that story because it offers such a clear example of the power of upside-down leadership when it starts with the leader and then radiates throughout the entire group. Coach Darin Owens had mastered the mindset that comes from consistently flipping your focus, and this allowed him to be the spark that led to record-breaking results. Likewise, this chapter captures the final breakthrough that occurs in an organization with genuine upside-down leadership. In interviewing many of the young men who played for the Knights, I heard what it was like to play for *both* coaches. As you will recall, Coach Smith led the team through a twenty-seven-game losing streak. Coach Owens, on the other hand, spearheaded the team's efforts to win the state championship in one year (his fourth time turning around a high school football program).

During each interview, the same comment was made. It summarizes the difference between typical organizations and exceptional, high-performance organizations. Under Coach Smith the players said they were "playing for themselves." It was all about their place on the team, personal notoriety, and being recognized over the intercom system. But under Coach Owens, 100 percent of the team members interviewed said they were "playing for each other." Under Owens, they were one man, one heart, and one mind, singly devoted to one purpose.

**Playing FOR Each Other**

This thought epitomizes where flipping your focus leads to, and what the ultimate team looks like. Is there a highest form of team? Is there a summit a leader can act as a catalyst to help his or her team achieve? There is. It's the team that embodies this thought: *It's not about me. It's about the person beside me.* That one thought becomes the stimulus for exceptional group performance, passion, and even profits. It changes everything and truly is at the very core of creating upside-down leaders at every level of an organization—not just at the top.

To develop this further, I must borrow other sports analogies. Sports are a wonderful mini laboratory for group performance, and many of the lessons that come from sports are relatable and transferrable to life and business.

The movie *When the Game Stands Tall* tells the story of the record-setting De La Salle Spartans. From 1992 to 2003 they compiled a record of 151 wins and no losses—perhaps the longest winning streak in sports history. Ironically, when he took the position of head coach, Bob Ladouceur had never coached high school football. But he had keen insight into young men and focused on fostering a unique culture of personal excellence coupled with unmatched unity. Ego was the enemy of teamwork, and he worked as hard at creating a culture of complete brotherhood as he did in establishing athletic prowess. In an opening scene of the movie, we observe a pre-game meeting where the starters all stand and publicly commit to their personal goal, game goal, and team goal. As one of the players rises to speak, you can vaguely read the logo on his shirt. It reads: It's not about the game. As the movie progresses, you wonder what that means. If it isn't about the game, what is it about? But then the message comes through in unmistakable terms. What allowed the Spartans to create such dominance on the field was their consistent effort to reinforce that success wasn't about the game—it was about the man beside them.

Another group that epitomizes this sense of selflessness are Navy Seals. After the death of Osama bin Laden, much was written about this mysterious group of warriors. One article in the *Wall Street Journal* piqued my interest. This article detailed the making of a Seal. It described the grueling physical endurance a Seal candidate must possess, the superhuman mental toughness, and the near-death situations to test their mental and physical fitness, including a drill called "drown-proofing" where it appears the Navy's goal is to kill you rather than keep you alive. But what struck me most were these words by the author, Lt. Cmdr. Eric Greitens, as he described those who made the final cut and became Seals:

*Some men who seemed impossibly weak at the beginning of SEAL training—men who puked on runs and had trouble with pull-ups—made it. Some men who were skinny and short and whose teeth chattered just looking at the ocean also made it. Some men, who were visibly afraid, sometimes to the point of shaking, made it too.*

*Almost all the men who survived possessed one common quality. Even in great pain, faced with the test of their lives, they had the ability to step outside of their own pain, put aside their own fear and ask: How can I help the guy next to me? They had more than the "fist" of courage and physical strength. They also had a heart large enough to think about others, to dedicate themselves to a higher purpose.*

### A Catalytic Turning Point

When is a team ready to achieve this? When is a team mentally, emotionally, and even spiritually prepared to make the shift to an unselfish organization? In my work, I've seen that it almost always happens in a catalytic moment—a moment of transition where what was once considered good enough is now viewed as not good enough moving forward. For the Seattle Seahawks, a locker room pep talk was such a moment. After being the 2014 Super Bowl Champions, the Seahawks were 3–3 midway through the next season. After their third loss, and second in a row, their coach Pete Carroll said words that changed everything and returned them to the Super Bowl that year. He told his team they were playing well together, but there was more inside they were capable of: playing **for** each other.

For the Hillcrest Knights of 2008, that moment of transition also came after a loss—the first loss of the season. Coach Darin Owens had led his team in hitting the reset button when he asked his players to stand up, look over both shoulders, and then look at him. With all the buildup that had happened with a new coach and new team spirit, and then to lose anyway, there was a sense of disbelief among the players. Still, after the game, the team hit reset together spontaneously while standing in a circle in the locker room and being led by their team captains. Once again, those young men looked over both shoulders and then at their captains. And this time there was no looking back. In the interviews with many of the players on that championship team, as they described the feeling that crept back on the field that night as they lost that first game, they all said the same thing: "We started playing for ourselves and not for the guy next to me. And when that happened, we were no longer truly a team." That night, after experiencing this loss, they buried this "me-focused" mindset for the rest of the season. They were now ready to become one.

## Reaching a Turning Point

In my work, I have personally witnessed entire teams hit the reset button, sometimes in a matter of two and a half days during a leadership retreat. And after that point in time, they never look back. High and low ropes "challenge courses" have been an extremely effective tool for inspiring this turning point, when they are expertly facilitated. Many times, I have seen clients at a point of extreme tension inside the organization—so great the groups were practically combustible—suddenly turn around and become united and unselfish. Within just a few brief days, old ways of doing things and old ways of working together become eclipsed by new vulnerabilities, expectations, sympathies, and loyalties. As they open themselves up to each other, face and overcome their physical and emotional fears, and then capture the lessons they experienced together, they hit the reset button—and then experience dramatic upside-down results. Businesses transform themselves from the inside out and, go on to achieve new levels of performance and profits.

## Upside-Down Leadership Comes First

To be clear, to reach this point, groups need to push the reset button collectively. Transformation can't take place unless upside-down leadership is being modeled. The unselfishness must reside within the leader first. You cannot have this level of team if you yourself are not striving to be this level of leader who is working to epitomize the core of an upside-down leader: unselfishness. It's bone-deep conviction that it's not about me—it's about my team. This paradigm is then modeled, taught, and spread throughout the group. A top-down, command and control organization has no chance of achieving this ultimate form of team unity because the context isn't even understood. The leader has not established the framework that would permit this type of unselfish organization to develop. But with the steps outlined throughout this book, this ultimate form of teamwork and team culture is within the reach of every upside-down leader.

**Case Study: The Abundance That Comes through Sharing**

Dr. Carol Pearson is a client who wondered if this statement was true. Four years ago, she purchased a specialty dental practice from a true control-type doctor. For over twenty-five years he had fostered the classic command, fear-based culture. As one of his former employees said, "I just kept my head down, did exactly what I knew he wanted me to do, and I didn't get in trouble."

When Dr. Pearson purchased this business, she realized quickly there was something more she wanted to do. She had different expectations for herself and her team. When she became my client, the first thing she did was read Covey's *Seven Habits of Highly Effective People* to discover the paradigm of abundance. We then began working through the specific skills outlined in *Flip Your Focus*. In the process, she aspired to be an upside-down leader. She then learned to spread ownership, clarify expectations, create a culture of participation, and show genuine appreciation. She then began working with her entire team to effect change. Trainings helped them hit the reset button, and they stepped onto the path toward becoming an upside-down organization of unselfish individuals who are looking out for the needs of their team. And while the members of her team are the very same people who worked with the first doctor (except for two new hires), their approach to work—and to each other—has changed. With their new, unselfish approach, they have set new records in business performance while enjoying their jobs, their patients, and their team like never before.

## A Simple Question with Profound Implications

To gauge whether a team is progressing toward this goal is very simple. It boils down to this: are the team members constantly asking the question "Who needs me now?" or are they asking the question "How can I relax?" A who-needs-me-now organization is full of team members, and even owners, who realize their mission is to help other team members fulfill their mission.

## The Ripple Effect into Hearts and Lives

Ultimately, upside-down leadership goes far past the needs of a business. It affects those involved in every aspect of their lives. Through your own act of influencing others in your leadership role and modeling a new and effective way of life, you move in your business (and in the lives of your employees) from success to lasting significance. You move from worrying about money to focusing on legacy, and you realize that in the end it's not about the business. Business is just a vehicle that permits us to see ourselves clearly. As I said in the opening, nothing brings us face-to-face with ourselves more than owning a business. Likewise, nothing brings team members face-to-face with themselves more than the challenge and opportunity that comes with being a part of an upside-down organization.

When the day arrives that our legacy is all that's left, when we are all contemporaries and death is the final chapter in our life here on earth, what will we be remembered by? Will it be the profits or the net income? Will it even be the customers served? Or will it be the lives of those who were in our care, part of our teams, and who changed because we changed, who grew because we grew, who became a part of an outstanding and exceptional "by design" culture?

Every member of a team arrives with gold inside of them, and that gold needs to be mined. The mining process requires skill, effort, and patience. Businesses take time acquiring gold because it is gold that allows them to pursue their mission. But this gold is temporary; it is fleeting. The true gold, to paraphrase Andrew Carnegie, is inside the souls of men and women. That is what the ultimate team creates. It's not just an organization that delivers outstanding results day in and day out, but an organization that creates outstanding people. And those outstanding people will not only ensure the success of the organization, but will also take that success and use it to transform everything they are a part of: from their family, to their church, to their neighborhood, to their community.

The ripple effect of an upside-down mindset is like a lattice of upside-down triangles, all connected to each other, all built upon each other, relying on each other, and knowing it's not about me—it's about the people next to me.

We are beings who are accustomed to social structure and the principle of sacrifice. We all want to be a part of something bigger than ourselves. At the core of our being we all want to contribute to something that fulfills the greater good. We just need to know how to do it and then have the foundation in place to finally reach this highest level of human engagement. Upside-down leadership lays that foundation, builds the superstructure on top of it, and ultimately creates the ecosystem where the truly unselfish team can flourish. What a marvelous, life-changing journey for everyone touched by this!

**Coach's Challenge**

1. Is your team playing for themselves or are they playing for each other? What are you doing to cultivate an organization of team players?
2. If your business needs to have a catalytic moment or turning point, what will you do to make it happen?
3. How can you use the mindset and skills taught in this book to become an upside-down leader?

4. Will you apply all the tools that this book has to offer into your life?

# Epilogue:
# The Case for Leadership

In closing, let me bring you back to a beautiful mountain lake where, standing on a beach with the sun just setting behind some sharp canyon walls, I was just about to be dragged underwater instead of launched airborne. As shared in chapter seven, my family had been invited to go parasailing behind a neighbor's ski boat, and after my three sons had gone – it was my turn to go. Unfortunately, the ride didn't start as planned. The reason for this mishap was twofold: the sun had gone behind the cliffs surrounding the lake so the light was growing dim. And, since I was the fourth person to be towed behind the boat, the tow-rope connecting the rider to the boat had become dark, muddy and blended into the beach. Both factors contributed to my Doug not being able to see the rope clearly enough to know the exact moment it was completely tight between us. His lack of clarity caused him to accelerate too soon, when there was still about ten feet of rope on the beach. And that lack of clarity created a profound ten-second crisis for me. But the clear expectations he outlined before we started overcame the crisis. The clarity he provided changed everything.

The clarity of thought that has come through this book can transform your life, your business, and all you touch. Repeatedly, I have seen it create order out of chaos, purpose out of frustration, and significance out of sheer survival. The clarity of understanding that business change begins with personal change, and then starting with the absolute commitment of not blaming, not becoming a victim, and learning that it's the lessons and not the losses. You then add to that accepting upside-down leadership is the ultimate way to create exceptional success within an organization.

You follow through by setting clear expectations, establishing personal and group accountability with genuine facilitated participation, targeted and appropriate appreciation that is tied to your values, and build a culture that is sustainable, and ultimately unselfish.

In the process, you will touch countless individuals through your example—the culture you fostered, the success you created, and especially the mentoring given. Oh, what a difference mentors make! It has been a privilege to share with you lessons they have shared with me. This book would not exist without the time and attention they took planting seeds of clarity and principle along the way.

The clarity of the actions and the paradigms presented will permit you to rise above the chaos you feel today, the sense of being totally underwater while everything around you is going faster and faster.

The steps described in this book make up the process that will help you get your feet in front of you. Get them there, keep them there, and then enjoy the greatest ride you will ever have. This ride—the ride that changes businesses, futures, and the lives of those you touch —is high adventure. The outcomes are record breaking but, more importantly, unforgettable.

**Coach's Challenge**

1. Describe the changes that have already taken place in you after reading this book. What do you want to do with these changes? How can you build on them to become the leader your business needs and your life is calling for?
2. Write a letter to your best friend a year from now. Describe the changes that have taken place in you and in your organization. What obstacles did you face? Who helped you overcome them? How have things changed from where they are today? How do you feel about them? What is next?

3. Put in writing a compelling vision of you as an upside-down leader. How do you communicate? How do you spend your time? And how does your organization feel and operate with you at this level of performance?
4. Who will you enlist among your peers to help create this transformation?
5. Who will you hire to coach you with your blind sides and allow you to grow even faster?
6. What will be the personal rewards for this progress in upside-down leadership to take place? What will be the rewards for your team and company?
7. What will be the penalties if this progress doesn't take place? How can you ensure these don't occur?

## About the Author

Bob is a team builder whose passion is developing genuine leaders and building high-performance teams. His firm, Spiel & Associates (www.SpielConsulting.com), transforms businesses by building leaders at all levels through a process of Transfacilitative Coaching™—acting as a catalyst for business owners and their teams to discover, connect, and commit to new levels of personal and team performance.

In his years of consulting and speaking, Bob has seen leadership can be taught and teams can be remade—what it takes is genuine desire, the willingness to be coached, and an unwavering commitment for growth.

Throughout his thirty-year career, Bob he has been called "Mr. Team" and has had the opportunity to take on tough turnaround situations as a hospital CEO, Surgical Center CEO, and as an Operations Director for two Fortune 500 companies where he led teams of up to 500 people while establishing world-class systems and cultures.

He now consults for dental practices and small businesses nationwide. He can be reached at Robert@SpielConsulting.com.

Made in the USA
San Bernardino, CA
05 October 2018